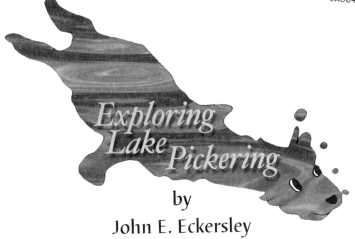

Exploring Lake Pickering

by
John E. Eckersley

with
Mark Comer
Nancy Eckersley
Daniel Savage
Leslie Stanbridge

Published by
John E. Eckersley

ISBN 0 9535862 2 7

Printed by
Maxiprint (York) Ltd, York, England

Foreword

As a walker, the idea of Christians as a 'pilgrim people', a people on a journey, has always appealed to me. As I travel round the Diocese, I often put my walking boots and jacket in the car boot which gives me the opportunity to snatch a little time in the countryside when my appointments are over. The landscape of the Diocese of York and especially of the Vale of Pickering tells the story of Christianity in this area through both buildings and landscape.

On the Lake Pickering Circuit, there are some remarkably beautiful church buildings, many of which are ancient and associated with particular saints or times in history. Whilst I am hesitant to pick out any in particular, the opportunity to walk into Lastingham and kneel in the silence of the crypt of the church, remembering St Cedd and the many pilgrims who have made that journey in the past, is one that I have always found to be profoundly memorable. The landscape, too, speaks of Christian witness – a particular example being around Rievaulx Abbey with its history as a Cistercian House with lands over many acres in the surrounding area. But as the modern day pilgrim or walker takes the time to visit the many parish churches, they will discover not simply a faith of the past, but a living faith of the present where people are seeking to engage creatively with opportunities for the church to foster community and witness to that same faith that took St Cedd and early Celtic missionaries on their journey so many centuries ago.

It is my hope that by using this guide you will not only enjoy the walks and the countryside but also have the opportunity to reflect prayerfully on your own life's journey.

+ Ʌ ⅃ Ǝ⅄ɴ:

David Ebor
Archbishop of York

Health Warning

When John Eckersley retired eighteen months ago from teaching Geography at St Aidan's CE School, we all breathed an enormous sigh of relief. No more of 'John's Jaunts' we thought. No longer any need to think of excuses why we might try to opt out of running all over Yorkshire in the charity sponsored 'walks' John dreamed up each year for Christian Aid. No more the need to feign broken legs, heart attacks or go on sabbatical leave to Australia in order to avoid being 'persuaded' to join in the fun.

Alas, we were mistaken. Last month John came to me and said, in his usual, terribly hard-to-say-no-to way: 'Tim, I've got a problem. I need some help. I've devised this new stroll round the Vale of Pickering and I've nobody to inaugurate it for me. You know I'd love to do it myself, but I'm getting a bit past it now. Do you think there's any chance of your getting some volunteers to do it – perhaps some of the staff at St Aidan's would be keen? After all, it's all for charity ...'

Then he added casually as an after-thought: 'Oh, by the way, this one's a bit longer than the 100-milers we used to do. In fact, it's 155 miles.'

And then there was the second after-thought: 'Oh, and I nearly forgot; can you sell a few hundred of the guide books at the same time? After all, it's all for charity ...'

Poor John! What could I say?

At St Aidan's we've had great fun in the past completing 'John's Jaunts' and we're eagerly looking forward to inaugurating this (surely his last?) marathon venture for Christian Aid on 10th May 2003.

Hope you too have a jolly jaunt!

Tim Pocock

Tim Pocock
(St Aidan's Charity Co-ordinator)
(still – amazingly – a friend of John Eckersley)

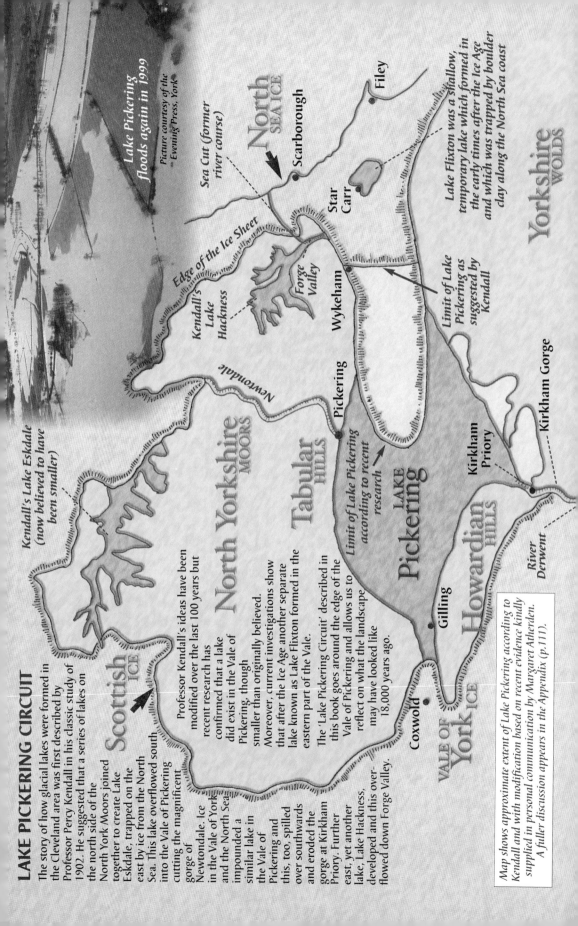

LAKE PICKERING CIRCUIT

The story of how glacial lakes were formed in the Cleveland area was first described by Professor Percy Kendall in his classic study of 1902. He suggested that a series of lakes on the north side of the North York Moors joined together to create Lake Eskdale, trapped on the east by ice from the North Sea. This lake overflowed south into the Vale of Pickering cutting the magnificent gorge of Newtondale. Ice in the Vale of York and the North Sea impounded a similar lake in the Vale of Pickering and this, too, spilled over southwards and eroded the gorge at Kirkham Priory. Further east, yet another lake, Lake Hackness, developed and this overflowed down Forge Valley.

Professor Kendall's ideas have been modified over the last 100 years but recent research has confirmed that a lake did exist in the Vale of Pickering, though smaller than originally believed. Moreover, current investigations show that after the Ice Age another separate lake known as Lake Flixton formed in the eastern part of the Vale.

The 'Lake Pickering Circuit' described in this book goes around the edge of the Vale of Pickering and allows us to reflect on what the landscape may have looked like 18,000 years ago.

Lake Pickering floods again in 1999

Picture courtesy of the Evening Press, York

Kendall's Lake Eskdale (now believed to have been smaller)

Scottish ICE

North Yorkshire MOORS

Newtondale

Edge of the Ice Sheet

Kendall's Lake Hackness

Forge Valley

North SEA ICE

Sea Cut (former river course)

Scarborough

Filey

Star Carr

Wykeham

Lake Flixton was a shallow, temporary lake which formed in the early times after the Ice Age and which was trapped by boulder clay along the North Sea coast

Yorkshire WOLDS

Pickering

Tabular HILLS

LAKE Pickering

Limit of Lake Pickering according to recent research

Limit of Lake Pickering as suggested by Kendall

Kirkham Priory

Kirkham Gorge

River Derwent

Howardian HILLS

Gilling

Coxwold

VALE OF York ICE

Map shows approximate extent of Lake Pickering according to Kendall and with modification based on recent evidence kindly supplied in personal communication by Margaret Atherden. A fuller discussion appears in the Appendix (p.111).

Landscapes

The Vale of Pickering is a lowland area with Kimmeridge Clay as its bedrock but with later glacial sands and gravels, moraines, lake clays and post-glacial alluvium and peat on the surface. Around the edge of the Vale, the Lake Pickering Circuit traverses four different hilly areas: the Howardian Hills, the Tabular Hills, the North Sea coastal cliffs and the Wolds.

The Howardian Hills

The limestones and sandstones of the Howardians are part of the Corallian division of Jurassic age rocks which formed originally in warm, shallow water. These rocks make a horseshoe-shaped outcrop around the Vale of Pickering. As well as forming the Howardians, they also make up the Hambleton, Tabular and Hackness Hills. The Howardians are the only area of Jurassic limestone in northern England to be given Area of Outstanding Natural Beauty (AONB) status and contain eight SSSIs and nearly fifty other nature conservation sites.

The Tabular Hills

Although they form part of the North York Moors National Park, the flat-topped Tabular Hills make up a distinct geological unit. Like the Howardians they are made of Corallian hard sandstones and limestones. On the north side they present a spectacular scarp slope. On their south side there is a major fault which runs along the southern edge of the hills and here the limestones dip under the younger clay rocks of the Vale of Pickering. This means that water which flows down southwards from the permeable limestone on to the impermeable clays of the Vale comes to the surface as a line of springs. Villages along the A170 follow this line of springs.

As the limestones are permeable, the rivers which flow over them are subject to considerable variations in flow and both the Rye and Derwent are known to have 'swallow holes' down which water disappears. This means there may well be less water lower down the course than higher up the valley. There are some intricate patterns of subterranean caverns and one old story even tells of how a goose wandered underground between Kirkbymoorside and Kirkdale.

The large number of dry dales which dissect the Tabular Hills are generally assumed to have been formed at the end of the Ice Age when underground water courses were still frozen so that the rivers had to flow on the surface. Yet in 1910 a cloud burst caused a spectacular flood in the normally dry valley of Wy Dale.

The Coast

Along the coast we follow the Cleveland Way and walk along the hummocky deposits of boulder clay left by the ice sheets as they moved down from Scotland and across from Scandinavia. The unstable clay regularly slumps down the cliff face, sometimes necessitating path diversions and in more extreme cases causing buildings like Scarborough's Holbeck Hotel to collapse. In Cayton Bay we may be lucky and find granite pebbles, originally from Scotland, or even agates and semi-precious stones washed out by the sea from the soft clay. When we come to Filey Brigg, the steep slopes of the clay have been eroded by rain water into a 'badlands' landscape of deep gulleys and sharp ridges whilst at the seaward end the clay has been washed away altogether by the sea. The Brigg itself is formed of very hard calcareous grit but underneath is a bed of oolitic limestone. Large chunks of this limestone have been thrown up by the sea on to the Brigg and at Carr Naze erosion has carved the oolite into delightful little amphitheatres called 'doodles'.

The Wolds

The Wolds are made of chalk which, like the limestone of the Tabular Hills, is permeable and so there is a lack of water on the surface. We may see the occasional dew pond, constructed to hold rainwater for farm animals, but it is easy to feel isolated in the deep dry valleys which score the landscape of low, undulating hills. Where springs come to the surface at the foot of the north-facing chalk scarp, we find a line of villages strung out along the A64-A1039 in a similar way to those located along the A170 on the north side of the Vale.

Lake Pickering Circuit and Circular Walk Distances

WALK LOCATIONS	LPC DISTANCE (miles)	LPC (TOTAL) (miles)	CIRCULAR WALK (miles)	CIRCULAR (TOTALS) (miles)
1 KIRKHAM PRIORY - CHANTING HILL	2.4	2.4	10.0	10.0
2 CHANTING HILL - CONEYSTHORPE BANKS	5.3	7.7	10.1	20.1
3 CONEYSTHORPE BANKS - SLINGSBY BANKS	1.5	9.2	10.9	31.0
4 SLINGSBY BANKS - HOVINGHAM	3.2	12.4	12.0	43.0
5 HOVINGHAM - CAWTON	1.6	14.0	10.4	53.4
6 CAWTON - GILLING - PARK WOOD	3.5	17.5	10.5	63.9
7 PARK WOOD - COXWOLD - BYLAND - AMPLEFORTH	9.1	26.6	10.7	74.6
8 AMPLEFORTH - SPROXTON	5.8	32.4	10.7	85.3
9 SPROXTON - HELMSLEY	2.8	35.2	6.2	91.5
10 HELMSLEY CIRCUIT	13.7	48.9	14.0	105.5
11 HELMSLEY - POCKLEY	2.1	51.0	9.4	114.9
12 POCKLEY - NAWTON - KIRKDALE	4.7	55.7	9.8	124.7
13 KIRKDALE - KIRKBYMOORSIDE	1.7	57.4	9.2	133.9
14 KIRKBYMOORSIDE - APPLETON-LE-MOORS	3.4	60.8	10.7	144.6
15 APPLETON-LE-MOORS - WRELTON	3.8	64.6	10.5	155.1
16 WRELTON - PICKERING	3.2	67.8	12.1	167.2
17 PICKERING - THORNTON - ELLERBURN	4.7	72.5	9.1	176.3
18 ELLERBURN - GIVENDALE	3.3	75.8	10.5	187.5
19 GIVENDALE - ALLERSTON - EBBERSTON	4.0	79.8	9.8	196.6
20 EBBERSTON - WYDALE - SAWDON	4.1	83.9	10.4	207.0
21 SAWDON - BROMPTON - HUTTON BUSCEL	5.6	89.5	12.0	219.0
22 HUTTON BUSCEL - WEST AYTON - FORGE VALLEY	8.1	97.6	11.1	230.1
23 FORGE VALLEY - FALSGRAVE MOOR	6.1	103.7	10.1	240.2
24 FALSGRAVE MOOR - OSGODBY (and SCARBOROUGH)	5.2	108.9	11.4	251.6
25 OSGODBY - GRISTHORPE	3.4	112.3	6.7	258.3
26 GRISTHORPE - MUSTON (and FILEY)	2.6	114.9	12.0	270.3
27 MUSTON - RAVEN DALE	3.2	118.1	10.6	280.9
28 RAVEN DALE - BINNINGTON BROW	4.7	122.8	11.0	291.9
29 BINNINGTON BROW - SHERBURN	4.1	126.9	9.3	301.2
30 SHERBURN - EAST HESLERTON	2.4	129.3	10.0	311.2
31 EAST HESLERTON - KNAPTON PLANTATION	2.3	131.6	10.2	321.4
32 KNAPTON PLANTATION - THORPE BASSETT	3.6	135.2	9.2	330.6
33 THORPE BASSETT - SETTRINGTON	3.4	138.6	11.1	341.7
34 SETTRINGTON - NORTON	4.3	142.9	10.6	352.3
35 NORTON - MALTON - LOW HUTTON	8.2	151.1	12.1	364.4
36 LOW HUTTON - KIRKHAM PRIORY	3.5	154.6	13.0	377.4
(KIRKHAM - HOWSHAM)	(3.3)	(157.9)	(7.0)	(384.4)

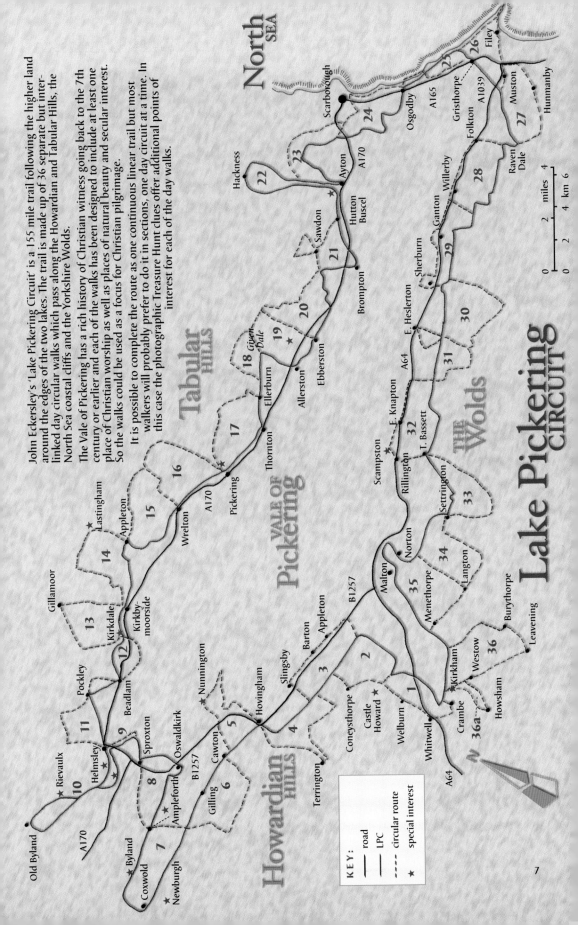

John Eckersley's 'Lake Pickering Circuit' is a 155 mile trail following the higher land around the edges of the two lakes. The trail is made up of 36 separate but inter-linked day circular walks which pass along the Howardian and Tabular Hills, the North Sea coastal cliffs and the Yorkshire Wolds.

The Vale of Pickering has a rich history of Christian witness going back to the 7th century or earlier and each of the walks has been designed to include at least one place of Christian worship as well as places of natural beauty and secular interest. So the walks could be used as a focus for Christian pilgrimage.

It is possible to complete the route as one continuous linear trail but most walkers will probably prefer to do it in sections, one day circuit at a time. In this case the photographic Treasure Hunt clues offer additional points of interest for each of the day walks.

Lake Pickering CIRCUIT

North SEA

Tabular HILLS

VALE OF Pickering

Howardian HILLS

THE Wolds

KEY:
— road
— LPC
--- circular route
★ special interest

Cradle of Christianity

Christianity came to the Vale of Pickering in the seventh century though – who knows – there may have been Christians among the Roman soldiers garrisoned at Malton three centuries earlier because there were certainly Christians in York at that time.

Before the Norman Conquest

Bede in his 'History of the English Church', written in the early 8th century, tells of the establishment of a Celtic monastery at Lastingham some time around 655. At the same time nuns from the abbey at Whitby founded a monastery at Hackness. There are churches dedicated to St Oswald at Filey and at Oswaldkirk and it is possible that the saintly King Oswald, accompanying St Aidan on his missionary journeys from Lindisfarne, landed at Filey and then rode along the 'Street', the old Roman road linking the villages along the south side of the Vale, before founding the church at Oswaldkirk around 640.

The earliest village churches were set up as 'minsters' or mission centres from which a community of priests taught the Christian faith in surrounding areas. Two of these minsters were at Stonegrave and Kirkdale. Local churches were almost certainly built of wood, with stone crosses standing in the churchyards. Parts of crosses from this early period are built into the walls of later pre-conquest church towers like those at Hovingham and Middleton.

The coming of the Vikings brought a period of destruction: churches were burnt and the monastery at Lastingham was sacked. Later, however, as the Vikings became Christians themselves, churches were rebuilt and around the Vale of Pickering a remarkable number were erected in the century before the Norman conquest: Appleton-le-Street, Hovingham, Kirkdale, Middleton, Ellerburn and Hackness date from this period.

Middle Ages: Churches

Following the Norman Conquest in 1066, a huge wave of new church building began. By the end of the 11th century stone churches were being erected in most villages. These usually consisted simply of a nave and a chancel. Side aisles and chantry chapels were added later. In the Norman period the doorways were often enriched with elaborate carving, as at Barton-le-Street. The interiors were decorated with wall paintings like the splendid murals which survive in Pickering church. However, little remains of the stained glass which filled every window, though there is some at Coxwold and at Winteringham.

Middle Ages: Monasteries

The period following the arrival of the Normans also saw a great flowering of monastic life. In 1077 a group of **Benedictine monks** re-established the monastery at Whitby. A year later some of them left to re-found the monastic house at Lastingham; others went to Hackness though quickly moved back to Whitby. At Lastingham the monks began to rebuild their church but had only completed the east end, with the crypt beneath, before moving to York to set up St Mary's Abbey.

Cistercian monks came to the area in 1131 when twelve brothers from the monastery of Clairvaux in France settled at Rievaulx at the invitation of Walter l'Espec, a wealthy nobleman of Helmsley. Another group of Cistercians founded the abbey at Byland.

While the Cistercians were building Byland, a community of **Augustinian canons** was being established at Newburgh, about three miles away. The community life of the canons was akin to that of the monks, with a strict ordered regime of worship, study and work but in addition the canons were involved in caring for the people in the surrounding parishes. The two communities worked together to drain the land and the monks' canals and fish ponds can be seen today.

Another Augustinian house was set up at Kirkham. Walter l'Espec, who had been responsible for establishing the Cistercian abbey at Rievaulx, also founded this priory and there were close relationships between the two houses. At one time it was suggested that the Kirkham canons might become Cistercians, but this never happened.

The only order of monks to originate in England was the **Gilbertines**, founded by Gilbert of Sempringham who established the mother house at Sempringham in Lincolnshire. Most Gilbertine monasteries were double houses for men and women but the monastery at Old Malton, founded in 1150, was only for men. Old Malton's Priory Church is, apart from the unfinished church at Lastingham, the only monastic church in the area to survive the Reformation as a parish church, albeit in a truncated form.

The Reformation

The reign of Henry VIII in the 16th century brought the dissolution of the monasteries, the confiscation of their property and the destruction of their buildings. Some foundations like Newburgh were converted to private houses; monasteries near towns were quarried for building stone; houses like Byland and Rievaulx were left roofless and gradually crumbled away. Rievaulx was later preserved in the 18th century as a picturesque ruin and the grass terraces above the abbey were levelled to provide fine views of the ruin through the trees.

In the reign of Edward VI, who came to the throne in 1547, there was a wave of destruction which obliterated wall paintings, smashed stone altars and destroyed rood screens. Then later the churches were gradually re-furnished with high pews to protect their occupants from draughts during seemingly interminable sermons. Some 17th century furniture remains in Coxwold church, though the fine pews have been lowered.

Quakers, Methodists and Roman Catholics

The founder of the **Quakers**, George Fox, preached in Ryedale in 1651 and groups of Quakers began to worship in farms and orchards. The earliest Quaker meeting house in the area is at Kirkbymoorside and dates from 1691. There is a lovely Quaker burial ground, dating from 1675, in the valley at Lowna north of Gillamoor.

In the following century **Methodism** spread rapidly in the area and John Wesley preached in the Vale of Pickering over a period of some forty years. By the end of the 18th century the Methodist congregation at Helmsley had grown to 1800 members and chapels had been set up in many villages.

Despite the upheaval of the Reformation, the old Catholic faith never entirely died out in the area and recusant families continued to worship in private. But the rebirth of **Roman Catholicism** in Ryedale dates from the foundation of Ampleforth Abbey in 1802. The community of Benedictine monks at Dieulouard in France had for 200 years been sending missionaries to serve the Roman Catholic population in England. However, during the French Revolution their monastery was confiscated and the monks fled to England, eventually obtaining land at Ampleforth. They soon established an Abbey School and in the 20th century have built a fine new Abbey Church.

Nineteenth century

A fresh wave of church building and restoration took place in the 19th century. An increased emphasis on the Communion service led to the transformation of church chancels. Stalls were provided for robed choirs and organs were installed. Western galleries were taken down and old high box pews replaced. Often the plaster was scraped from the interior walls, taking with it the remains of medieval wall paintings. New stained glass windows replaced the clear glass which had been put in after the medieval glass had been smashed. Most of the churches in the Vale of Pickering were restored and some were largely rebuilt. Some villages like Appleton-le-Moors acquired fine new churches for the first time. By the end of the 19th century most of the village churches were in excellent structural condition.

Today

Recent years have seen the different Churches working more closely together in the Vale of Pickering. Despite problems of vandalism and theft, most of the buildings remain open for visitors and many provide admirable guides which help to remind us both of the rich spiritual heritage and the priceless architectural treasures which the Vale is privileged to enjoy.

WALK 1
KIRKHAM PRIORY – CHANTING HILL

Map: Explorer 300
S.E.P.: Kirkham Priory (735658)
Lake Pickering distance: **2.4 miles**
Circular walk distance: **10.0 miles**
Shorter walks:
    North loop   2.5 miles;
    Middle loop   6.5 miles;
    South loop   4.3 miles
Special interest: Kirkham Priory, Pretty Wood

This first walk of the Lake Pickering Circuit (LPC) includes a section of the River Derwent overflow gorge, several attractive villages and the locally popular 'Bluebell Walk'.

From the car park at Kirkham Priory we walk down the road to cross the River Derwent on the ancient Kirkham Bridge. Ignoring the Centenary Way (CW) signs which direct us off right before the level crossing, we carry on and then turn off a few metres after the crossing. The route goes parallel to the railway until we veer left slightly upslope through a patch of bracken into Ben Wood. Waymarks direct us and, though a bit boggy in places, the path is generally clear.

At (1) we carry on straight over the road and after a short climb there is a very pleasant stroll through Ox Carr Wood with good views down to the river in its gorge below. The p.r.o.w. goes through a gate at (2), follows the beech hedge to a big gap, goes though the gap and takes the tarmac to a magnificent redwood tree (try punching the trunk). We pass through another hedge on the right and then turn left on to a side road. This takes us through Crambeck village to the A64. Crossing with care, and bearing slightly right, we follow the CW waymarks through the gate and round the edge of Gillylees Wood.

From (3) marker posts show the way over ploughed arable land and then we follow a tall hedge to the path crossing at (4). Here we go right to another path junction at (5) where we turn left through the gate and continue to Todd Wood. The path enters the wood and we follow it (look out for King Oak) to the junction by the Four Faces folly and Pretty Wood. We bend left and this stretch of the route makes up part of the local 'Bluebell Walk' on account of its glorious springtime displays.

Towards the end of the wood (6), we go left down the steep slope of East Moor Banks, cross Moorhouse Beck and then follow the bridleway into Welburn. Going over the main road, we bear slightly left as we walk up to St John's Church.

Leaving the church, we go back a few metres down the lane and take the path on our left. Waymarks soon direct us round the school and we go up the slope, crossing a ploughed field, into a small copse. From there we are led through Monument Farm and, after two right-angle turns at signposted field corners, we come to the path crossing at (7). Here we turn left and, keeping the hedge on our right, soon reach the old road into Whitwell-on-the-Hill. A right turn brings us to the Parish Church.

From the church we take the path immediately next to the lych-gate and walk by the field edge to the A64. **We cross with extreme care.** Then on the other side we turn right and use the pavement for about 400m to bring us to Cliff Lane (8). This broad track takes us to a T-junction at (9) where we go left and continue by the hedge down to Crambe, swinging right to arrive at St Michael's Church.

The path continues on the south side of the church, through part of the graveyard, on to the lane at (10). Here we go right, then left over the cattle grid at (11), and follow the waymarks up the hill before turning right to reach the stile giving entrance to Oak Cliff Wood. We walk just inside the trees on a soft bed of coniferous needles and then after leaving the wood continue down beside a high blackthorn hedge to the road (12). Turning right for just 40m we then turn right again for 20m to the footpath leading down left into the trees. This takes us back to the road into Kirkham.

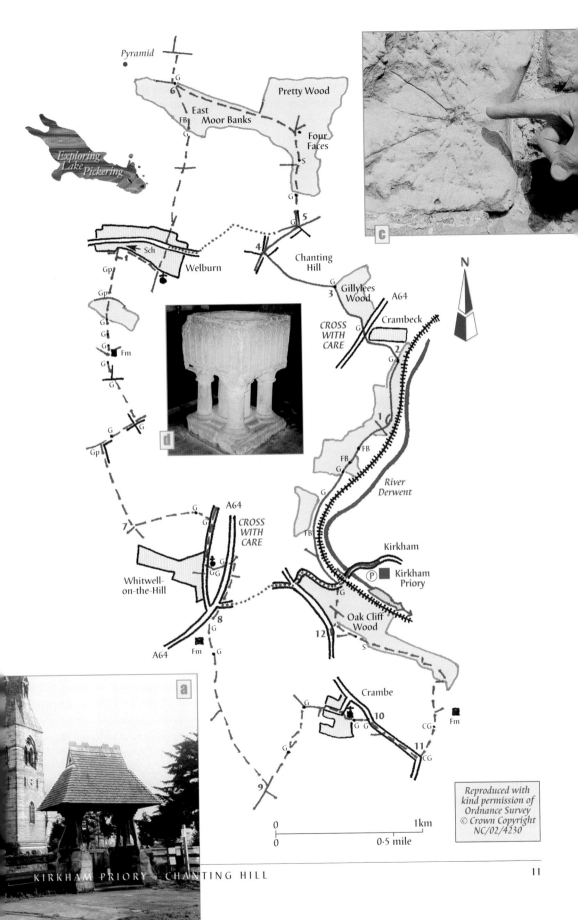

Pyramid

Pretty Wood

East
Moor Banks

6

FB

G

Exploring Lake Pickering

Four
Faces

S

G

G **5**

4

Welburn

Sch

Gp

Chanting
Hill

Gp

G

G

G

Gp

G

G

G

G

Gp

c

N

Gillylees
Wood

G **3**

A64

CROSS
WITH
CARE

G

Crambeck

2

G

1

FB

FB

G

G

*River
Derwent*

FB

d

7

G

G

A64

CROSS
WITH
CARE

G

G
GG

Kirkham

Whitwell-
on-the-Hill

P

Kirkham
Priory

G

8

G

Oak Cliff
Wood

A64

Fm

G

12

S

Crambe

G

10

a

G
G G

CG

Fm

11

CG

G

9

0   1km

0   0·5 mile

Special Interest - WALK 1

Kirkham Priory

Kirkham Priory was founded around 1122 by Walter l'Espec, nobleman of Helmsley, who later founded Rievaulx Abbey. He set up a house for Augustinian Canons who lived a monastic life but also worked in the nearby parishes. The priory church served both the canons and the parish.

The splendid 13th century gatehouse can be enjoyed from the roadside. It is decorated with shields of the community's founders and benefactors and with a number of fine carvings. These include George and the dragon on one side of the entrance and David and Goliath on the other.

There is more to be seen of the priory buildings than we might at first think. From the gateway the surviving corner of a magnificent 13th century choir (or chancel area) gives some idea of the original splendour of the church. The nave, however, which was used by the parish, was both small and dark.

Normally the dormitory would have been on the first floor but because the priory was built on a sloping site overlooking the River Derwent, the dormitory is on the same level as the chapter house. The canons presumably had to pass through the cloister at night instead of entering the church by night stairs directly into the transept.

Parts of the refectory walls still stand with a fine 12th century doorway and the remains of a beautiful laver, the washplace outside the refectory door. This had a piped water supply, with taps.

Churches: St John's Church, Welburn was built between 1859 and 1865 in the style of the 1300s and stands prominently above the village. **Whitwell** has another Victorian church (1858-1860) also dedicated to St John. There is a tiled dado and beautiful stone inlaid work in the font and pulpit. **St Michael's Church, Crambe** has a fine Norman font, 15th century tower, 17th century carved pulpit and interesting carvings on the tower archway. The exterior walls show fascinating evidence of the changes which have taken place over the centuries.

Kirkham Priory

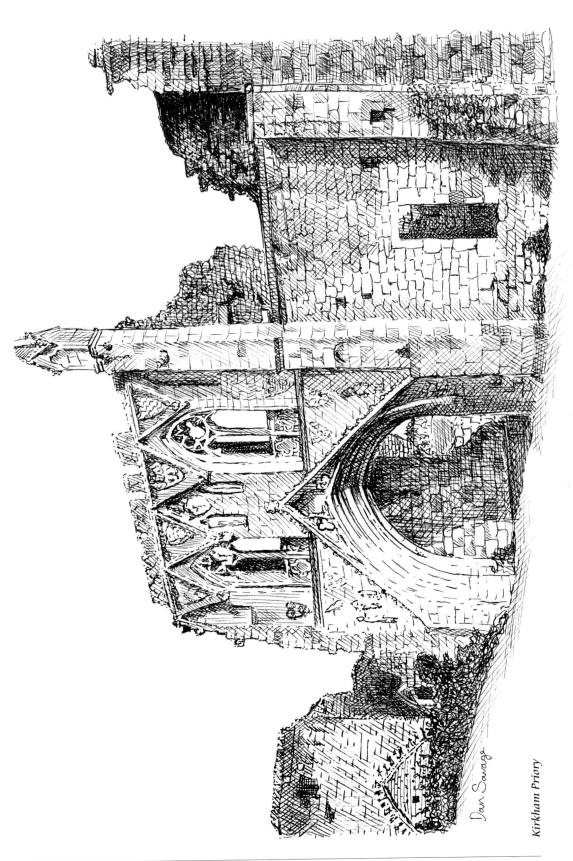

Dan Savage

Kirkham Priory

WALK 2
CHANTING HILL- CONEYSTHORPE BANKS

Map: Explorer 300
S.E.P.: Lay-by car park (707712)
Lake Pickering distance: **5.3 miles**
Circular walk distance: **10.1 miles**
Shorter walk alternatives: **8.3 miles;**
5.8 miles
Special interest:
    Castle Howard, Howardian Ridgeway

The LPC section of this walk joins and then follows the ancient ridge-top Earthwork along the crest of the main line of the Howardian Hills. The rest of the circular walk goes through parts of the Castle Howard estate and allows good views of some of its outlying buildings.

From the large roadside car park, we take the road through Coneysthorpe and turn right by the far end of the buildings at the gate and fingerpost (1). We follow the wider bridleway track forking right, not the footpath branching left.

At the edge of Ray Wood we turn left and then after about 300m turn right at the track junction (2). Then at (3) the path bends right again along the wood boundary and brings us to the Temple of the Four Winds. From here we go downhill to cross New River (really a very large pond) noting the Mausoleum away to our left and then, a little later, the Pyramid to our right.

The track takes us up to the tarmacked Centenary Way; we cross over and continue to East Moor Banks (4). We turn left in the wood and for the next mile or so retrace (but in the opposite direction) the route we took on Walk 1 and make our way past the Four Faces to the path junction at (5). Here we join the main LPC.

This time we go left down the valley side to Cram Beck. Crossing the stream, we bear slightly left and follow the field boundary up the opposite valley side and on to Hutton Hill. At the farm our path, signed to High Gaterley, turns left, goes through a gate, crosses a ploughed field and then bends left after the next gate. At (6) we turn sharp right and take the path gently downslope to the footbridge over the ditch and then up the hill to High Gaterley.

Turning right we carry on a little further to the next junction (7) where we go left along the

hedge side and then down Thackadale Lane to the turning at (8). We can continue straight ahead and do a short out-and-back detour to see the Holy Well in the trees a little way up on our left. Then we continue west to pass through the Alamo Trekking Centre before carrying on along the bridleway round the edge of Spring Wood to the bend at (9).

Here we are careful; it's easy to swing round left on the main track but we only do this if we are using the short circuit via Bog Hall back to Coneysthorpe. Otherwise we need to bend right and go through the gate leading up the steep hillside. A big zig-zag takes us to the road where we go straight over and follow the waymarks round Park House (now a small business park) on to the ancient track running along the crest of the Howardian ridge.

From here, we have one of the most attractive sections on the whole of the LPC. There is a good surface underfoot, views over the 'Lake' are extensive and we have the assurance of an ancient earthwork to protect us from marauding tribes attacking us from the south. We go as far as the fingerpost on our left (10) indicating the Centenary Way and here descend a sometimes slippery slope to the edge of the wood.

We need to turn left for a short distance to the waymarked gap before leaving the trees and following the grassy track back to Coneysthorpe. There should be time to look in **Coneysthorpe Chapel** before going back to our cars. The chapel was built in Georgian style with plain windows but was not erected until 1835. At the time of writing it was awaiting refurbishment.

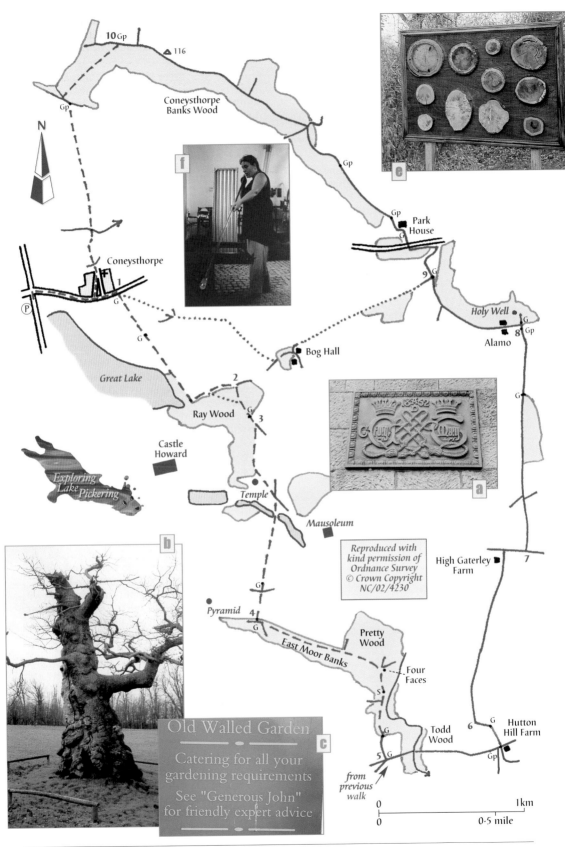

10 Gp

▲ 116

Coneysthorpe
Banks Wood

Gp

Gp

N

Gp

f

Coneysthorpe

1

P

G

Great Lake

G

2

Ray Wood

G

3

Castle
Howard

*Exploring
Lake
Pickering*

b

Temple

Mausoleum

Reproduced with
kind permission of
Ordnance Survey
© Crown Copyright
NC/02/4230

a

Park
House
Gp
G

9 G

Holy Well G
8 G Gp
Alamo

Bog Hall

G

High Gaterley
Farm

7

Pyramid

4
G

East Moor Banks

Pretty
Wood

Four
Faces

S

G

G

Todd
Wood

5 G

*from
previous
walk*

6 G

G

Hutton
Hill Farm

Gp

e

Old Walled Garden
c

Catering for all your
gardening requirements

See "Generous John"
for friendly expert advice

0   1km

0   0·5 mile

Special Interest - WALK 2

Castle Howard

Castle Howard is one of the nation's most treasured stately homes. It is possible to combine a visit to the 18th century house and its extensive collections of furniture, paintings, and sculptures with a visit to the Arboretum which opened in 1999. Jorvik Glassblowers are another recent attraction.

Castle Howard really owes its importance to three people in particular: Charles, third Earl of Carlisle, Sir John Vanburgh (1664-1726) and Nicholas Hawksmoor (1661-1736). When the Castle of Henderskelfe was seriously damaged by fire, Charles Howard decided to replace it with one designed by Vanburgh with assistance from Hawksmoor. Vanburgh was a playwright and what is amazing is that Castle Howard was the first building he had ever planned. Construction began around 1700 but when he died the building was still not finished and the later West Wing was the design of Thomas Robinson, the third earl's son-in-law.

Apart from the obvious grand scale of the project, several innovative ideas made Castle Howard special. It was the first private house in England to be built with such a large dome and the orientation of the house was quite different from the traditional setting. Instead of facing east and west, Castle Howard faces north and south with all the main rooms facing the south and so benefiting from maximum sunlight and warmth.

The route we take on our walk allows us to view a number of the buildings on the Castle Howard estate. We first pass the **Temple of the Four Winds** designed by Vanburgh. The domed building has four Ionic porticoes and the interior design is important because the walls are decorated with a type of artificial marble called scagliola and Castle Howard is believed to have been the first place in England where this had been used.

From the **New River Bridge** we can look in one direction to the waterfall and further on to the South Lake designed by Vanburgh. In the other direction we see the **Mausoleum,** thought by some to be Hawksmoor's finest work, though with design changes by others. The Earls of Carlisle and their families are buried in the crypt beneath the chapel.

A little further along the walk we spot the **Pyramid** over to our right. This contains a large bust of Lord William Howard (1563-1640) from whom the Castle Howard branch of the Howard family originates. He married Elizabeth Dacre and thereby acquired Naworth Castle, estates in Cumberland and Northumberland and the Henderskelfe Castle and Estate as well. William was 14 and Bessie 8 at the time of their 'marriage'.

Two areas of woodland at Castle Howard are of national significance. **Ray Wood**, described in 1563 as an area of 'fine young woodland' was almost entirely clear-felled during World War II but then replanted. Today Ray Wood is especially important for its rhododendrons, with 500 species and another 300 hybrids, as well as other rare trees and shrubs. James Russell gave his Sunningdale Collection of plants to Castle Howard when his collection was moved north from Surrey. A large number of the plants are the direct descendants, propagated vegetatively, from the originally introduced species.

Building on the success of Ray Wood, an **arboretum** has been established. There are over 180 different types of willow and a unique collection of Sorbus (rowans and whitebeams). Numerous plants have been grown from wild-source seed collected on expeditions around the world. The arboretum is undoubtedly of extreme value for species conservation and research. Together with Ray Wood, there are estimated to be over 6,500 different types of plants and the arboretum has a variety of habitats, with contrasting well-drained valley slopes as well as boggy valley floor.

There are both shorter and longer Tree Trails, with exceptionally helpful information leaflets, as well as the Furniture Makers' Walk. In the Visitor Centre there is a fascinating display of the different woods used through the centuries by British furniture makers.

Castle Howard

WALK 3
CONEYSTHORPE BANKS
- SLINGSBY BANKS

Map: Explorer 300
S.E.P.: Slingsby Church (697749)
Lake Pickering distance (excl that done
on Walk 2):   **1.5 miles**
Circular walk distance: **10.9 miles**
Shorter walk alternatives: **7.9 miles;**
                                 5.8 miles

Special interest:
    Howardian Ridgeway, 'Street' villages

Coming out of the church, the short walk goes left to the main B1257 road and then takes the track called Kirk Road to rejoin the long walk near (9). The two longer walks leave the church and go back to the village green, then bend right, and right again, to come to the hedged track at (4). This goes along field edges and then over a small paddock to the B1257 at Appleton-le-Street. A little further on, we use the roadside steps to take us up to the church.

From here the medium distance walk goes along the track called Appleton Lane up to the top of the main Howardian ridge. Those completing the full circuit walk continue through Appleton to the turn-off left (also called Appleton Lane)

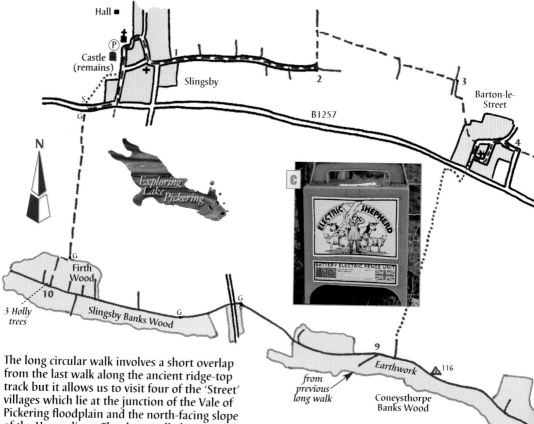

The long circular walk involves a short overlap from the last walk along the ancient ridge-top track but it allows us to visit four of the 'Street' villages which lie at the junction of the Vale of Pickering floodplain and the north-facing slope of the Howardians. The short walk does not include the repetition along the ridge.

Starting from Slingsby Church we walk south, noticing the remains of the castle on our right, and then turn left along The Green and go through the village to Green Dyke Lane (1). We take this road eastwards to (2) then follow the waymarks which lead us round Wandale Farm and along the line of telegraph poles to the two tracks at (3). We take the one on the far side of the hedge which brings us through Manor Farm and on to Barton-le-Street village green. Bearing right, we come to St Michael's Church with its superb Norman carvings.

at (5), go down the road to the fingerpost at (6) and then follow waymarks and stiles into Amotherby. Right and left turns take us to St Helen's church. From here we carry on to the B1257 and then turn left to the broad track at (7). Following this gently uphill for about a mile, we reach the Coneysthorpe road at (8). A right turn leads us to Park House where we meet the ridge-top route which we walked on Walk 2.

We continue along the crest of the ridge but this time, instead of going down the track at (9), we continue over the Slingsby road till we come to Firth Wood. There are several paths leading off right through the trees; the one we need is about 350m from the start of Firth Wood. We identify it by the three big holly trees on the right-hand side of the track. Turning off right into the trees, we go to the end of the wood, turn right for about 40m and then go left through the gate on the waymarked p.r.o.w. down to Slingsby. When we reach the main road we either use the path directly ahead or turn right along the road and come into the village that way.

Special Interest - WALK 3

The **Linear Earthwork,** sometimes known as the Entrenchment, which runs along the Howardian Ridge is of uncertain date but is generally believed to be of prehistoric age.

Malton Street was a Roman highway following the direction of the present B1257 Malton-Hovingham road. Remnants of the Roman surface can be found as scattered stones in a field near Slingsby.

Churches: All Saints, Slingsby is a large church, rebuilt in 1869, but still with something of a medieval atmosphere to it.

St Michael's, Barton-le-Street was likewise virtually rebuilt in 1871 but is still an exciting place with an amazing variety of Norman stone carving retained from the original building. The porch and main entrance are particularly impressive and inside is a fine carved Norman chancel arch and, under the roof, some of the carved corbel stones from the original building.

The site of **All Saints, Appleton-le-Street** was used for burials in Roman times and the church itself is pre-Norman with a tower built in late Saxon times around 1000 AD. Two aisles were added to the nave in the 12th and 13th centuries and the altar rails and communion table date from 1636. In the apex of the east window is a small piece of medieval glass showing the arms of the Greystock family, the barons of Henderskelfe (Castle Howard) in the 14th century.

St Helen's Church, Amotherby was another which was largely rebuilt in 1871 but it still has its Norman south door and 16th century tower as well as some Anglo-Danish carved stones, from before 1066, in the porch.

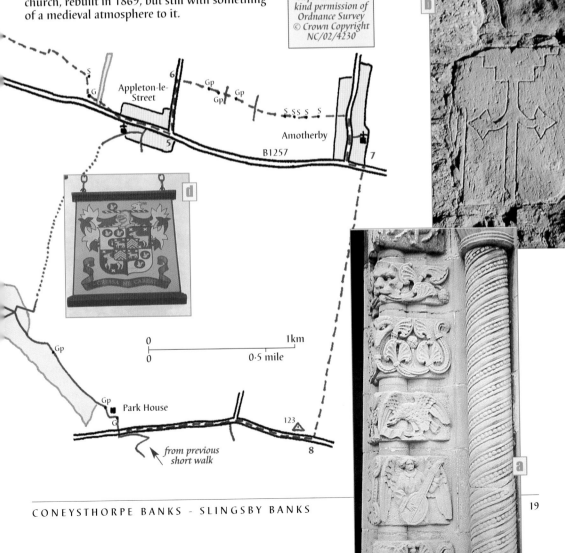

Reproduced with kind permission of Ordnance Survey
© Crown Copyright NC/02/4230

Special Interest - WALK 4

Hovingham Hall with its Riding School as the main focus, was designed and at least partially built by Sir Thomas Worsley, Surveyor-General, sometime between 1745-55. In the grounds of the Hall were found the remains of a Roman villa.

All Saints Church, Hovingham, was largely rebuilt in 1860 but the Anglo-Saxon sculpture and great tower, built shortly before the Norman conquest, remain and are worth investigation. High up on the tower is a wheel cross (10th century) and an earlier Anglian cross (probably 7th century). These are thought to have come from the remains of earlier churches which were on the site. There is also a Saxon doorway, now blocked, into the tower. The semi-circular door arch is in typical Saxon design with no central keystone. Behind the altar table in the recently re-ordered chancel is mounted another fine Viking cross.

Airyholme Farm is a centre for the breeding and export of rare and endangered sheep species. Castlemilk Mort, Leicester Longwools and Norfolk Horns are all found on the farm and it should be reasonably easy to spot the Hebridean Four-horned variety with its peculiar head-gear. Airyholme escaped the 2001 foot and mouth epidemic but the crisis stressed the need to have endangered species spread in a variety of locations. The farm's practice of exporting stock to the Continent helps to achieve this.

All Saints Church, Terrington, dates from the Norman period but if we look in the south aisle we can see a wall of Saxon herringbone work which was formerly the outside wall of the church. The north aisle arcade is 12th century, with carving resembling the work at Byland Abbey. In the 14th century the herringbone wall was broken into and an arch formed to give access to a chantry chapel. There is a notable 15th century tower with a recycled mass dial and 1767 sundial. Treasure hunters might like to find why 9470 is a significant number at Terrington Church ...

Special Interest - WALK 5

In the 1830s there were ambitious plans to develop **Hovingham Spa** as a rival to other Yorkshire resorts and one contemporary account tells how the waters at Hovingham contained sulphuretted hydrogen, carburetted hydrogen and nitrogen gases. Hot and cold baths, mud baths and a cold plunge bath were provided but the venture failed. Some of the springs, however, are just visible today from the track on the way to Cawton.

Apart from its tower, **Stonegrave Minster** looks from the outside like a Victorian church but the title 'Minster' recalls its foundation before 757 AD. The interior is of great interest: there are Norman arcades, medieval tombs, a beautiful 17th century chancel screen and a Jacobean pulpit. But the glory of the church is the collection of pre-Conquest carved stones, the earliest of which dates from the 9th century. The best preserved cross, almost complete, shows a priest-missionary going on his pastoral journeys.

All Saints Nunnington is a largely 13th century church entered by its medieval door. There is a Jacobean pulpit and some fine monuments including one to Thomas Jackson who died in 1760 and was well-known for 'his extraordinary performances on the turf'. And do read the story of brave Peter Loschy, valiant dragon slayer!

Nunnington Hall is a 17th century manor house owned by the National Trust and houses the Carlisle Collection of Miniature Rooms.

There has been a **water mill** in Nunnington since Anglo-Saxon times and the mill is mentioned in the Domesday Book. It was rebuilt in 1875 but stopped flour making in 1903 because of competition from bigger mills, though corn grinding continued. From 1920 to 1950 the millrace powered a small generator which gave electricity to Nunnington Hall.

Special Interest - WALK 6

Gilling Castle was founded in the 14th century by Thomas de Etton, though 'fortified manor house' is probably a better description than 'castle'. The basement, with massively thick walls, remains today but the house was largely rebuilt in the 16th century to include a magnificent Great Chamber. In 1885 the castle passed from the Fairfax family and was eventually bought in 1929 by Ampleforth College who use the building, now called St Martin's, Ampleforth, as their preparatory school. Visits can be arranged (01439 766000).

Holy Cross Church in **Gilling East** originated as a small Norman building but was enlarged with the later addition of aisles and a 15th century tower. There is an interesting 14th century tomb slab in the chancel and figures (1572) of Sir Nicholas Fairfax and his two wives in the south aisle. A Saxon stone cross stands on the south side of the church and grooves in the stonework by the south door may have been caused by Cromwell's men sharpening their weapons or perhaps by villagers honing their farm tools.

Holy Trinity Church, Yearsley was built in 1839 with a polygonal apse and lies just off the walk route.

Some Features of English Parish Churches

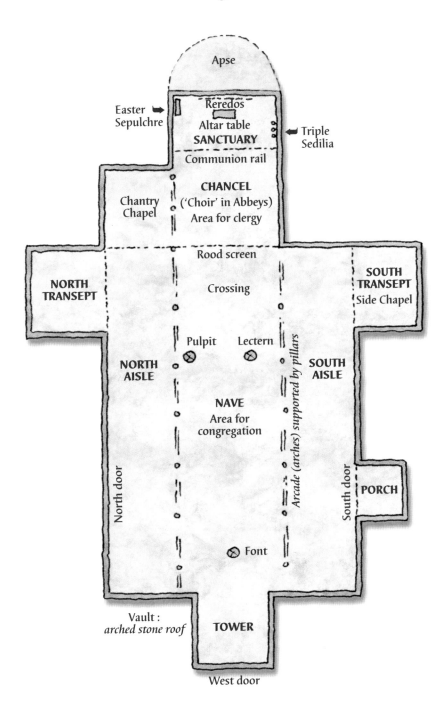

Apse

Easter → Sepulchre

Reredos

Altar table
SANCTUARY

← Triple Sedilia

Communion rail

CHANCEL
('Choir' in Abbeys)
Area for clergy

Chantry Chapel

Rood screen

NORTH TRANSEPT

Crossing

SOUTH TRANSEPT
Side Chapel

Pulpit

Lectern

NORTH AISLE

SOUTH AISLE

NAVE
Area for congregation

Arcade (arches) supported by pillars

North door

South door

PORCH

Font

Vault : *arched stone roof*

TOWER

West door

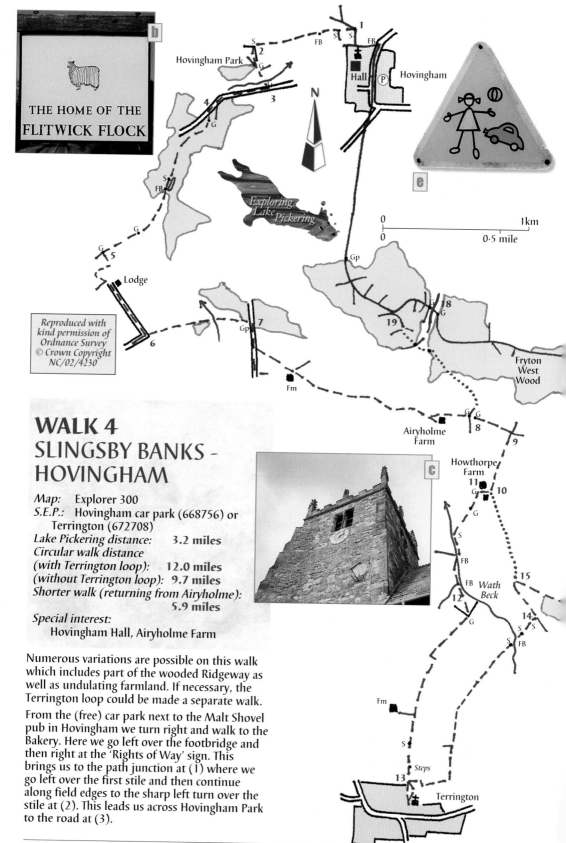

THE HOME OF THE
FLITWICK FLOCK

Hovingham Park

Hall · P · Hovingham

N

Exploring Lake Pickering

0 _____ 1km
0 _____ 0·5 mile

Lodge

Reproduced with
kind permission of
Ordnance Survey
© Crown Copyright
NC/02/4230

Fm

Fryton
West
Wood

Airyholme
Farm

Howthorpe
Farm

WALK 4
SLINGSBY BANKS –
HOVINGHAM

Map: Explorer 300
S.E.P.: Hovingham car park (668756) or
Terrington (672708)
Lake Pickering distance: **3.2 miles**
Circular walk distance
(with Terrington loop):   **12.0 miles**
(without Terrington loop): **9.7 miles**
Shorter walk (returning from Airyholme):
5.9 miles

Special interest:
Hovingham Hall, Airyholme Farm

Wath
Beck

Numerous variations are possible on this walk
which includes part of the wooded Ridgeway as
well as undulating farmland. If necessary, the
Terrington loop could be made a separate walk.

From the (free) car park next to the Malt Shovel
pub in Hovingham we turn right and walk to the
Bakery. Here we go left over the footbridge and
then right at the 'Rights of Way' sign. This
brings us to the path junction at (1) where we
go left over the first stile and then continue
along field edges to the sharp left turn over the
stile at (2). This leads us across Hovingham Park
to the road at (3).

Fm

Steps

Terrington

Now we turn right and walk to the bend in the road. Avoiding the gated pull-in and then ignoring the first track on our left, we turn off left at the finger-post on the second track 80m further on (4). This grassy path passes a clump of redwood trees before crossing a narrow planked footbridge and then continuing along the ditch to the stile at (5).

The p.r.o.w. now turns left, bends right and then left again to take us on past Hovingham Lodge. At the road corner (6) we branch left on a firm earth track to (7). Here we go right on the road to the sign for Airyholme and then take this track to the farm with its rare and endangered breeds of sheep.

The path bears left immediately before the farm buildings and comes to the ditch called Wath Beck (8). Here the short walk turns off left alongside the beck but the main walk continues straight on to the track crossing at (9) and then turns right up to Howthorpe Farm (10). At this point the middle distance walk bears left on the Ebor Way while the long walk turns right to the gate at (11).

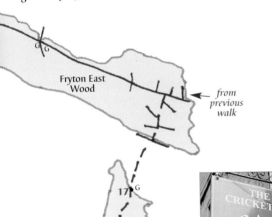

Fryton East Wood

from previous walk

17

Thurtle Wood

16

At the gate we turn left and go downhill and then at the next gate must cross diagonally over arable land to the stile in the far corner. Carrying on along Wath Beck, we soon cross over a footbridge and then quickly reach another footbridge at (12). Here the way is not too obvious: we aim diagonally up the slope to the gate in the field top corner. From here navigation is easy and we bear right and follow field edges into Terrington.

Having admired the church, we retrace steps to the finger-post (13), turn right on the Ebor Way

for two fields and then go left along field boundaries all the way back up to the wide track at (14). Waymarks indicate along which side of the hedge we should walk. Then turning left up the incline, we come to the path junction where the medium length walk joins in (15).

Bending back right, we follow a wide bridleway along the top of the ridge through Waite Wood and on to the junction at (16). We need to be watchful here; there is no waymark but an opening in the trees takes us to a half-gate and then the route is clear. Open woods provide attractive scenery but we avoid all branching tracks and carry on to the open gate at (17). Crossing pig farm country, we come to Slingsby Banks Wood and again keep to the main track up to the top of the ridge.

We have now rejoined the main Lake Pickering route along the crest of the Howardian ridge. Turning left, our way continues adjacent to the ancient hilltop earthwork which we encountered on Walks 2 and 3. The track is good except where it has been disturbed by heavy logging machinery.

Leaving the wood temporarily at (18), we cross a small patch of rough grazing and go over Wath Beck before entering the trees again through the gate immediately ahead of us. The woods are again delightful for walking and we stay once more on the main track, avoiding all side routes, until the major crossing point at (19) where the short walk and Ebor Way join in. We turn right and are led through the trees to the edge of the Estate woodland and from there we have a straight walk back into Hovingham.

THE CRICKETERS
BAR
FOOD
CAR PARK

a

d

1870.
Let thy widows trust in ME.

f

WALK 5
HOVINGHAM – CAWTON

Map: Explorer 300
S.E.P.: Hovingham car park (668756)
   or Nunnington (666791)
*Lake Pickering distance (excl that done
   on Walk 4):*   **1.6 miles**
Circular walk distance: **10.4 miles**
   (excl link to Walk 6)
Shorter walk alternatives:
   South loop   **6.3 miles;**
   North loop   **4.4 miles**
Special interest:
   Stonegrave Minster, Hovingham Spa,
   Nunnington Hall

This is a figure-of-eight walk which easily splits
into two smaller circuits. One loop focuses on
Stonegrave Minster and the other on
Nunnington Hall and the River Rye.

Leaving the car park next to the Malt Shovel pub
in Hovingham, we turn right and walk through
the village to the bend in the road by the bakery.
Here, turning left, we cross the footbridge over
the beck and go between the houses until we are
directed right at a notice board. At the stile (1)
by the cemetery we take the main bridleway.
This is the Centenary Way and forms a wide
track, 'improved' in parts with stone chippings,
which takes us past the site of Hovingham Spa
to Cawton.

At Cawton we turn right and must follow the
road at least as far as (2). Here we can leave the
tarmac and follow the p.r.o.w. along the hedge
before making our way over two ploughed fields
to the road corner at (3). Alternatively we may
prefer to stay on the road round to (3). Then we
use the fieldside track to take us past the pond
(look out for heron) to (4). Bearing diagonally
right we aim for Church Farm and, though the
p.r.o.w. goes through the farmyard, the
recommended route keeps to the edge of the
field before turning right through a gate and
then up a ladder stile into the churchyard.
Stonegrave Minster demands investigation and
there is an excellent information leaflet inside
the church.

We exit from the churchyard by the main
entrance and then turn back left on the B1257
going slightly uphill to the bridleway at (5).
Here we leave the road but then at (6) the track
divides. Those opting for the shorter walk bear
right and continue along the foot of the woods
to Caulkleys Grange. The longer route forks left,
up the steep sunken track to the top of the
ridge.

Assuming we are doing the longer walk, we get
fine views north and south until we come to the
path junction at (7). Here we turn left and go
down the wide bridleway to Nunnington
Church (8). We carry straight on into the village
and then turn right to Nunnington Hall.
Whether or not we decide to visit the Hall, we
should look out for the peacocks around the
property.

Turning right on the road and then left at the
High Orchard fingerpost, the waymarked path
then takes us right and left and then along the
side of the Hall's high garden wall. By the wall
end, we bear left down to the weir on the River
Rye and then continue through Mill Farm. From
here to Ness Bridge the path follows a straight
line, generally staying close to the riverside.

At Ness Bridge we join the road and turn right
to West Ness, bending right again to the road
junction at (9). We go straight across and take
the bridleway known as Caulkleys Lane. This
leads us over the path crossing at (10) and then
along the main ridge of Caulkleys Bank to the
road at (11).

Now there is a steep descent on the tarmac to
the lower path at (12) where the short walk
joins in. Here we turn left along the path at the
foot of Scroggy Wood and continue to Caulkleys
Grange.

The p.r.o.w. goes right and follows the farm
drive. It is then waymarked over arable land to
the footbridge at (13) after which we cross
another field (heavy clay in winter!) to Marrs
Beck (14). Turning right, we are soon able to
cross this wide ditch before going round the
field edges to yet another footbridge and then
the main B1257 road. Turning left, the last half
mile or so is along the roadside back to
Hovingham.

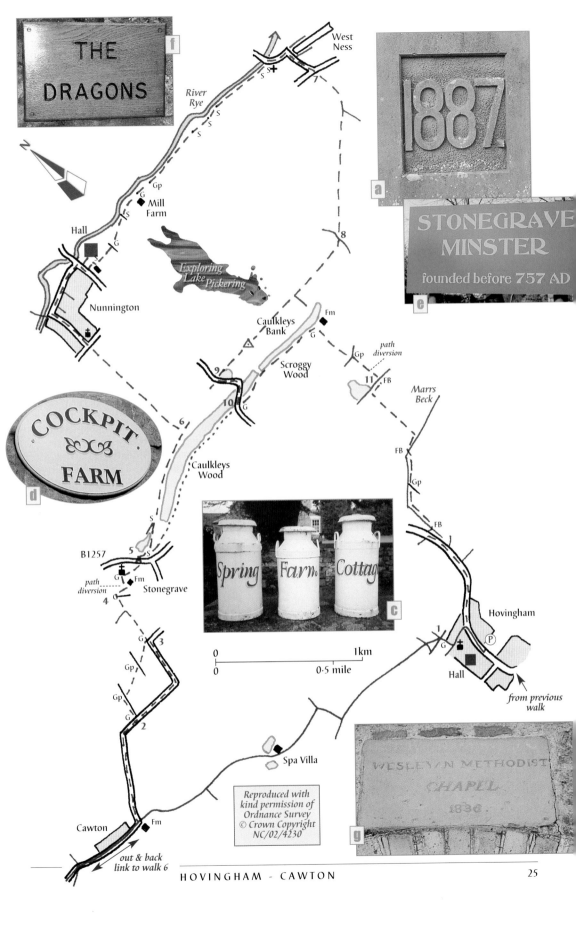

THE DRAGONS

West Ness

River Rye

S +

S

S

Gp

G   ◆ Mill
Farm

S

Hall   G

■

S   ◆

Nunnington

Exploring Lake Pickering

8

1887

a

STONEGRAVE MINSTER
founded before 757 AD

e

◆ Fm

Caulkleys   G
Bank

△   Gp   *path diversion*

Scroggy
Wood   11 / FB

9   *Marrs Beck*

10   G

6   FB

COCKPIT FARM

d

Caulkleys
Wood   Gp

FB

S

B1257   5
S

path diversion   G   ◆ Fm

4   Stonegrave

Spring Farm Cottage

c

Hovingham

1
G   �△   P

Hall

G   3

Gp

from previous walk

Gp
G   2

0 ———————————— 1km

0 ———————— 0·5 mile

◆ Spa Villa

WESLEYAN METHODIST CHAPEL 1836

g

Cawton   ◆ Fm

out & back link to walk 6

Reproduced with kind permission of Ordnance Survey © Crown Copyright NC/02/4230

WALK 6
CAWTON - GILLING - PARK WOOD

Map: Explorer 300
S.E.P.: Gilling East (616771) or
         Yearsley (585744)
Lake Pickering distance: **3.5 miles**
    (incl link to Walk 5)
Circular walk distance: **10.5 miles**
    (incl link to Walk 5)
Shorter walk alternative
    (along road):   **5.5 miles**
Special interest: Gilling Castle, Park Wood

This circuit involves some walking along quiet country lanes but there is the consolation of two attractive woodlands and there are fine views across the Coxwold-Gilling Gap to Ampleforth and the hills beyond. Ampleforth Abbey and the Forestry Commission generously allow walkers to use the route described but this concession in no way indicates any general right of public access.

It is possible to park in Cawton but space is limited and so the recommended start is from Gilling. We take the lane due westwards from the village crossroads and soon pass the miniature railway on our right and the track on our left leading up to Gilling Castle, now Ampleforth preparatory school.

The quiet road leads us along the edge of the valley drained by the Holbeck stream with a steeply wooded slope up on our left.

At Park House (1) we continue on the p.r.o.w. through the 'Private' property round to the Lower Fish Pond (2). There is a slight diversion of the p.r.o.w. but a clear track takes us through the mixed deciduous and coniferous Park Wood to the Higher Fish Ponds (3).

From here we use a concessionary route, kindly allowed by Ampleforth Abbey. Continuing straight ahead, we soon turn right at the T-junction (4) and then keep on the main track round and up to Piper Hill (5). Here we ignore the three tracks on our right and carry on up to the gatehouse by the road junction (6). (Here a possible short cut turns left on road back to Gilling East.)

We cross over the road and follow the B1363 to the crossroads at Grimston Grange (7) where we turn left and go as far as the gate into the F.C. wood (8). Entering the wood, we turn immediately right and keep to the main track as far as the T-junction at (9). Here we must turn right, walk to the road, turn left and then left again at the junction (10) and continue as far as the p.r.o.w. on our right at (11).

Walking left of the fence and then following the edge of another F.C. plantation, we come to the corner of the wood at (12). We take the p.r.o.w. going straight ahead, over the pasture, through a strip of wood and over another field to the two gates leading to the road. Going left we follow the tarmac to the fingerpost (13) opposite Cold Harbour.

From here we cross over pasture to Coulton Lane and then bear left and walk as far as the track to Stocking Hill Farm. This takes us through the farmyard and waymarks direct us down to a footbridge over a ditch and then over an arable field to the track called Green Lane (14). We go right on this track, up and over the ridge of Cawton Heights, to the edge of Cawton (15). From here there is a short stroll on the road back to Gilling, with good views of Ampleforth Abbey ahead of us over to our right.

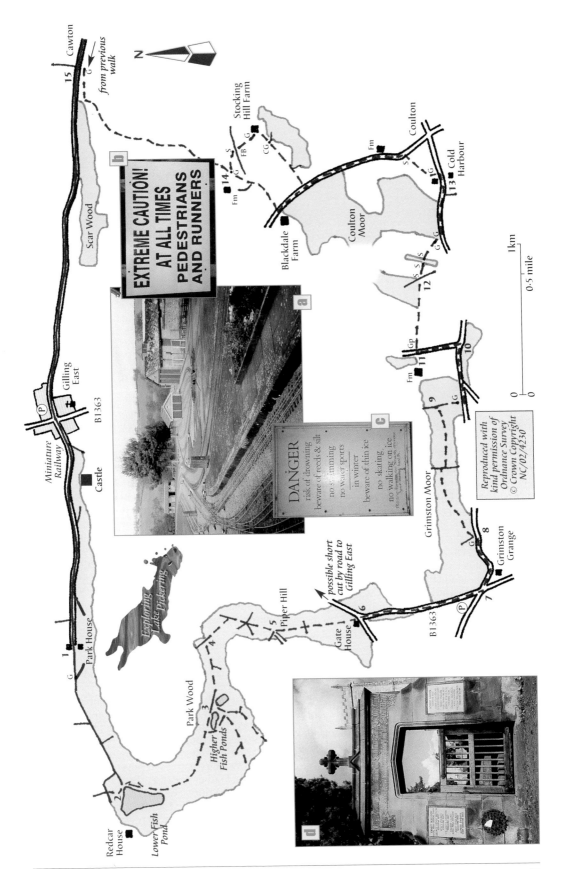

N

Cawton

from previous walk

15

G

Scar Wood

Stocking Hill Farm

S

G

FB

14

G

CG

S

Fm

G

Fm

Coulton

Blackdale Farm

Coulton Moor

Fm

S

G

13

Cold Harbour

G

G

12

S S

S S

G

EXTREME CAUTION!
AT ALL TIMES
PEDESTRIANS
AND RUNNERS

b

a

Exploring Lake Pickering

Gilling East

P

B1363

Miniature Railway

Castle

Park House

G

1

2

Redcar House

Lower Fish Pond

Park Wood

3

Higher Fish Ponds

4

5

Piper Hill

Gate House

possible short cut by road to Gilling East

6

7

P

B1363

8

G

Grimston Grange

9

G

Grimston Moor

Fm

10

11

Gp

DANGER
risk of drowning
beware of reeds & silt
no swimming
no water sports
in winter
beware of thin ice
no skating
no walking on ice

c

d

Reproduced with kind permission of Ordnance Survey © Crown Copyright NC/02/4230

0   0·5 mile   1km
0   1km

Byland Abbey

Byland Abbey

A group of Cistercian monks left Furness Abbey in Cumbria in 1138 and settled at Hood Grange, near Thirsk. Finding the site too small, they moved to Tylas, a couple of miles above Rievaulx in the Rye valley. Not surprisingly, problems arose because the two monasteries could hear each other's bells and the Furness monks were obliged to move once more, this time to Stocking, up on the hills not far from Sutton Bank. Gradually the community was becoming wealthy through gifts of land and while remaining at Stocking, sent lay brothers to drain the land at Byland where they were then able to build the largest and in some ways the most impressive Cistercian church in Yorkshire.

From the road we see a long line of identical round-headed window openings in the low outside walls of the church and with a little imagination we can envisage something of the splendour of the huge building, 100 metres long and constructed in what was at the time the most 'modern' style. The remains of the west wall, with its magnificent rose window, and of the south transept wall give some idea of the height of the church.

Like the abbey church at Rievaulx, the church at Byland was divided into the lay brothers' choir in the nave and the monks' choir further east.

The transepts were aisled and the east end very spacious. Large areas of fine floor tiles form one of the unique treasures of Byland.

The cloister was larger than that at Rievaulx but the buildings round it are less complete. One feature occurring at Byland but not at Rievaulx is the lay brothers' lane which runs alongside the cloister on the west side and was evidently a place where the lay brothers could talk without disturbing the silence of the cloister. Extensive parts of the lay brothers' buildings remain.

The small museum enables us to see the quality of the stone carving in the church as well as an exhibition of some of the floor tiles. There is also a map of the canals constructed by the monks of Byland and the Canons of Newburgh in order to drain the land and to create fish ponds.

Newburgh Priory is open to the public at selected times in summer (check on 01347 868435) but the lake is always visible from the roadside. Newburgh hides a secret: does it contain the body of Oliver Cromwell? After his daughter Mary had taken possession of her beheaded father's corpse, she transferred it to Newburgh Priory. She had married Viscount Fauconberg and the Fauconberg family owned the Augustinian Priory so it was assumed the remains would be safe from any further desecration. Later, a tomb was revealed but, despite numerous requests, it has never been opened. So the mystery remains.

St Michael's Church, Coxwold, dating from the 15th century, is of outstanding interest and is one of the two Yorkshire churches with octagonal towers. Inside the church there is a fine oak ceiling (c.1420), medieval stained glass and a musicians' gallery constructed originally in the 18th century. Box pews and pulpit also date from the 18th century. The chancel is unique, with its long communion rail stretching westwards because the Fauconberg monuments took up so much space.

Shandy Hall in Coxwold was the house to which the novelist Laurence Sterne came as vicar in 1760. Here, in his 'philosophical hut' he finished writing 'Tristram Shandy', a book which won him fame but also censure from those dismayed at the earthiness of the cleric's writing. After his death in London, stories spread that his body had been stolen by body-snatchers who had sawn off the top of his skull. His supposed remains are now re-interred in Coxwold.

Dan Savage

Byland Abbey

WALK 7
PARK WOOD - COXWOLD - BYLAND - AMPLEFORTH

Maps: Explorer 300 & Explorer OL 26
(& a tiny part of Ex299)
S.E.P.: Ampleforth (585782) or
Byland Abbey (548790) or
Coxwold (536773)

Lake Pickering distance:	**9.1 miles**
Circular walk distance:	**10.7 miles**
Shorter walk alternatives:	**5.6 miles;**
	7.3 miles

Special interest: Byland Abbey, Newburgh
Priory, Shandy Hall

This walk represents the furthest westward extension of the LPC. We cross the divide between east and west-flowing streams, reach the western end of the Coxwold-Gilling Gap and then start walking eastwards along the edge of the North York Moors National Park. The main focus of historical and ecclesiastical interest is the remains of Byland Abbey but the walk also allows a visit to Shandy Hall in Coxwold as well as a view of Newburgh Priory. We may therefore wish to plan our start and finish according to whether we intend stopping at any of these locations. For the description of the circular walk we shall assume a start from the Millennium Green in Ampleforth where there is space for a limited number of cars.

From the Millennium Green we take the p.r.o.w. which runs SSE from the side of the second house on Mill Lane. This continues for about a mile to the track (1) in front of the Lower Fish Pond. Here we turn right, following the track past Redcar House and then the field path to the road at (2). A right turn takes us to Thorpe Hall Open Farm where we can break our walk and visit the 'Farming Flashback' collection of old farm machinery. We are allowed access through the farmyard to join the p.r.o.w. which leads us on to the Colley Broach Road (3).

Turning right, we can follow this little-used lane, passing the short-cut turn-off (4), all the way to the road junction at (5). However, the preferred alternative, shown on the accompanying map, is to use two short sections of public path across fields. A quick out-and-back detour gives the opportunity to catch sight of Newburgh Priory (or to count the ducks on the adjacent lake).

We walk into and through Coxwold village, noting St Michael's Church and perhaps visiting Shandy Hall, home of Laurence Sterne. A little further along the road, we turn right at the indicator post and walk across Town's Pasture; this can be boggy in wet weather. Some minor diversions have been made to the p.r.o.w. but we follow the waymarks in a general NNE direction, turning left, then right and continuing up to the second footbridge at (6).

Here we alter direction and, walking NE, follow the waymarks past a recently established plantation and over another footbridge up to Cams Head. Turning right, there are now six stiles to cross before we come to the road at (7). A left turn takes us to Byland Abbey.

Those wishing for a more leisurely study of the Abbey and its museum may pay at the kiosk for entry to the precinct. Otherwise we continue on the road round to the stile at (8), cross over the field and obtain excellent views from the path of the carefully maintained Abbey remains.

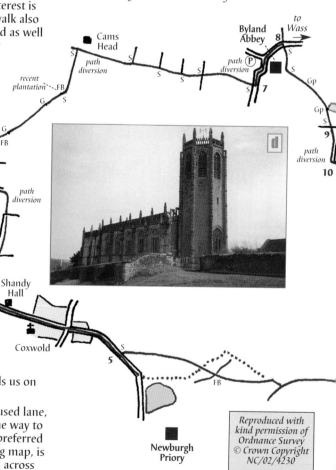

Swinging left after the next stile, the path is a little unclear but runs along a terrace, cuts through a gap in a straggly line of trees and then bears right over flatter ground to the stile at (9).

Waymarks now direct us on the diverted path up to the hilltop ruin at (10) and from here we turn left following the field edge. There are fine views and particularly interesting is Craykeland Wood directly ahead. This hill has been identified as the moraine left by the Vale of York's glacier.

Crossing the third stile (11) we follow the line of waymarked telegraph poles up and over the side of Hessle Hill towards Wass Grange but we turn off right before the farm and make for the gate at (12). Then at the following gate, we take the p.r.o.w. forking left, again going up and over the hillside. Waymarked stiles lead us to Carr Lane (13).

Bearing right, the road takes us into Ampleforth and we turn sharp right at (14) to follow a pleasant beck-side path leading down to Mill Farm where we go left on the road back to our start.

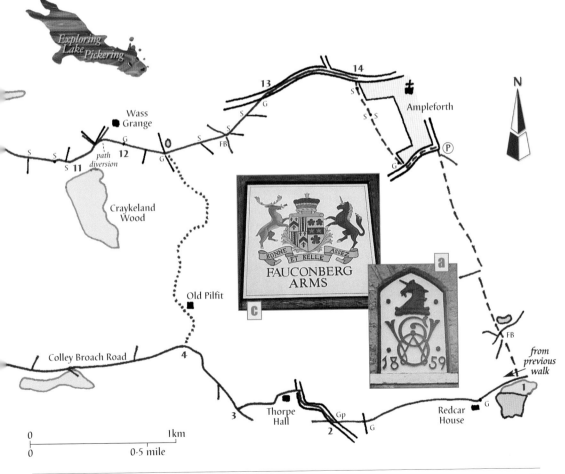

WALK 8
AMPLEFORTH - SPROXTON

Map: Explorer OL 26
S.E.P.: Ampleforth (585782) or
Sproxton (618815)
Lake Pickering distance: **5.8 miles**
Circular walk distance: **10.7 miles**
Shorter walk alternatives: **7.2 miles** and
7.2 miles

Special interest:
Ampleforth Abbey, Studford Ring

This walk takes us past Ampleforth Abbey and along the Ebor Way to Sproxton. The return route goes through farmland and forest before visiting the prehistoric circle at Studford Ring and then descending to Ampleforth.

Parking in Ampleforth is not easy so we start, as on Walk 7, from the Millennium Green sports field. We retrace the last part of Walk 7 to Mill Farm and then follow the beck to the main road and almost directly opposite a fingerpost indicates the p.r.o.w. (1). The path goes past the side of Brook Cottage, immediately to the right of the garage, along the edge of the back garden and then up alongside the beck into the trees. We turn right at the stile, cross the stream and then go to the path junction at (2).

Ignoring the waymark directing us downhill, we continue instead on the higher p.r.o.w., with its fine views down to Ampleforth and beyond, over nine field boundaries (stiles or hedge gaps) to (3). Here the p.r.o.w. turns at right angles up the slope to Windmill Farm. However, the

landowner very kindly allows LPC walkers to continue to the gate on the road at Beacon Bank. Please remember that this is a goodwill gesture and in no way implies any general right of public access. From there it's a short walk along the road to the gate at (4).

We go down through the trees, above the old disused quarries and Ampleforth Abbey, touch the road at (5) and then head up the slope again to Whin Grange Farm. Turning right on Stockings Lane we follow the road to the path diversion (6) and then go right again along the hedge side. At the trees (7) we go through a small gate, turn left and then walk along the top edge of the wood. (This is a delight in springtime with an abundance of woodland flowers.)

To visit the church we can take a path on our right down to the road and walk through the village. Otherwise we stay at the top of the trees and when we reach (8) we go left (near the big mirror) then right at the B1257 and walk to the junction at (9). Turning left, we now join the Ebor Way, tarred at first, and take this to Sproxton. Navigation along field boundaries is easy on the waymarked route, though at (10) we are careful as we bear left, first through a small gate and then through a second, big gate.

Just before Sproxton, the LPC turns off right (11) on the Ebor Way. The day circular walk carries on through the village to St Chad's Church. At the church we go left downhill along the B1257 and at the first bend turn right along Hag Lane. We follow this quiet road gently upslope to Holly Bower Farm, pausing now and again to look back eastwards across Lake Pickering.

The path continues, doing a slight right-left jiggle at (12), to Pry Rigg Plantation. Access is allowed by the Forestry Commission although at first we follow a public bridleway, turning left, then sharp right (14), along a delightful grassy ride to High Street (15).

Going right for about 100m we then take the path on our left across farmland to Studford Ring. This ancient circle is accessible from the path.

From Studford, our general direction is south and we follow waymarks and stiles gradually downhill to the path crossing at (2). From there it's a just a short way back to the main road where we turn left, then right down Station Road and past St Hilda's Church to our starting point.

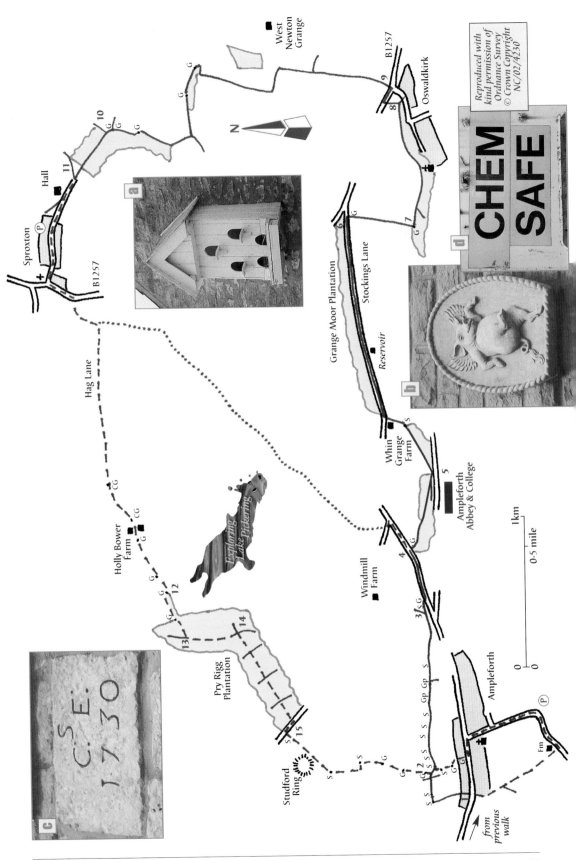

Sproxton

Hall

B1257

West Newton Grange

10

11

N

B1257

9

8

Oswaldkirk

CHEM SAFE

a

d

Grange Moor Plantation

Stockings Lane

Reservoir

6

7

Whin Grange Farm

S

b

5

Ampleforth Abbey & College

Hag Lane

Exploring Lake Pickering

Holly Bower Farm

CG

CG

G

G

12

Windmill Farm

4

G

3

S G

1km

0.5 mile

13

14

Pry Rigg Plantation

15

S

c

C. S. E. 1730

Studford Ring

S

S

S

S

S

S

S

Gp Gp

G

G

Ampleforth

P

Fm

from previous walk

Reproduced with kind permission of Ordnance Survey © Crown Copyright NC/02/4230

Special Interest - WALK 8

Ampleforth Abbey and College

In 1802 the community of Benedictine monks who had spent nine years as exiles from Dieulouard after the French Revolution were given the house which had been built by Ann Fairfax of Gilling Castle for her chaplain, himself a monk of Dieulouard. Soon after, in 1808, Ampleforth School was opened and since then building has gone on continuously. Before the Second World War, as well as the infirmary, an indoor rifle range was constructed. At the time of writing there are 90 monks in the Ampleforth Community, though 32 of them live away from Ampleforth and do parish work in other parts of the country. Other monasteries have been set up at Osmotherley and near Preston at Bamber Bridge. Even more impressive, perhaps, has been the establishment of Ampleforth centres at St Louis in the U.S.A. (1955) and in Zimbabwe (1996). This work of outreach from an established home base is reminiscent of earlier centuries when the great monasteries of Yorkshire were engaged in similar mission.

The line of buildings at Ampleforth, best viewed from the south, is dominated by the Abbey Church. This was designed by Sir Giles Scott, the architect of Liverpool's Anglican Cathedral, and replaced the previous church which had been completed in 1857. Visits can be arranged (01439 766889).

Studford Ring has not been properly investigated but has been tentatively dated as belonging to the immediate pre-Roman Iron Age. It is not likely to have been a defensive site because the ditch is on the inside of the mound. It occupies a prominent position on the upper valley side, though it is not as high as the land a little to the north-west.

St Hilda's Church in **Ampleforth** village, was almost entirely rebuilt in the late 19th century but still has its Norman doorway and font.

St Oswald's Church, Oswaldkirk was probably founded in the 7th century, though there is little in the present building dating from before the Norman period. The 1886 restoration included the east window glass showing the story of St Oswald.

St Chad's Church at **Sproxton** was originally the Elizabethan chapel of West Newton Grange but there it fell into ruin and was used as a farm shed until it was rescued in 1879 and rebuilt, stone by stone, in its present location in Sproxton. There is a fine reredos behind the altar table and a small panel of medieval glass (c.1420) above the font.

Special Interest - WALK 9

Helmsley Castle

It is thought likely that an early castle was built here in the 12th century by Walter l'Espec, the founder of Kirkham and Rievaulx. But the oldest stonework visible now dates from around 1200 when the castle was held by Robert de Roos. The castle, on a low ridge of limestone, relied on massive earthwork banks and ditches for its defence. Despite its impressive appearance, the castle enjoyed a relatively uneventful history. After numerous changes in ownership, Charles Duncombe acquired the castle and its estate after the death of George Villiers.

During the Civil War the castle came under siege from the Parliamentarians in 1644. Royalists from Skipton and Knaresborough attempted to lift the siege but were unsuccessful and had to withdraw. Then the castle surrendered but was afterwards 'slighted' to make sure it could not be used again.

All Saints Church, Helmsley is another church almost entirely rebuilt (1866-1869) by the Victorians but the Norman south doorway and chancel arch remain. Stained glass and modern mural paintings tell the story of the church in these parts and as well as viewing scenes from Helmsley's history we can learn about St Aidan and Walter l'Espec. The church guidebook advises us 'do not miss the dragon, the mice and the slave's yoke'. Canons from Kirkham Priory used to serve the church in the Middle Ages and Canon's Garth, built behind the church for their accommodation, serves as the present day vicarage. C.N.Gray, vicar from 1870-1913, is reputed to have been able to 'hold his own in a boxing match against any of his parishioners with one arm tied behind his back'.

Helmsley Castle

WALK 9
SPROXTON - HELMSLEY

Map: Explorer OL 26
S.E.P.: Sproxton (618815) or
        Helmsley car park (610838)
Lake Pickering distance: **2.8 miles**
Circular walk distance: **6.2 miles**
Special interest: Helmsley Castle and Church

This is only a short circuit but there is the opportunity to explore Helmsley market town with its castle and church and some may wish to visit Duncombe Park at the same time. Parking is limited in Sproxton but it is possible to find space for a few cars near the former village hall (now a joiner's workshop) without blocking driveways. Alternatively, some may prefer to park in Helmsley and walk the circuit in reverse. Treasure Hunt clues may be found in Sproxton village.

We walk from the joiner's workshop past the older hall to join the Ebor Way (EW) at (1). Here we fork left and take the waymarked track past Low Parks Farm over gently rolling farmland to the River Rye. However, we don't cross the river but, turning left, stay on the nearside bank and walk towards Helmsley. (On our return we shall use the opposite, east, side of the river.)

The path essentially keeps to the riverside, though where the O.S. map shows it crossing the water, we stick to dry land. The river is delightfully clean, sand martins sweep around their nesting holes ... and geography teachers have a field day talking about river meanders, ox-bow lakes and cut-off channels.

In spring time there is a wonderful show of yellow celandines and primroses and when we enter the strip of woodland (2) there's a gorgeous carpet of wood anemones and wild garlic.

At (3) the p.r.o.w. goes over a stile and keeps about 70m to the right of the boundary fence to reach the A170. Turning right on the road, we go over the River Rye and into Helmsley market square. Walkers wishing to

explore the town should certainly visit the church and the castle.

To go back to Sproxton we walk south on the A170 (Bridge Street), turn left down Ryegate and then after about 200m go right at the EW sign (4). The road continues past Thomas the Baker and through the light industrial estate to the path junction at (5). Here we turn right and follow the waymarks which direct us to the riverside Ebor Way path. Passing the sewage works (I wonder why the official EW is not on the other side of the river?) we soon swing left and then at (6) cross a stile. We must bear right through two gates – not under the disused railway tunnel – on what now classes as a bridleway. This leads past the fish farm to the footbridge over the Rye and from here we re-trace our route back to Sproxton.

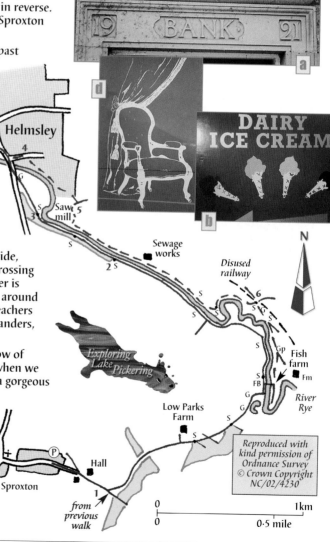

Reproduced with kind permission of Ordnance Survey © Crown Copyright NC/02/4230

Special Interest - WALK 10

Rievaulx Abbey

This magnificent Cistercian abbey was founded in 1131 and within thirty years the original community of twelve had expanded to include 140 monks and 600 lay brothers. Daughter houses were set up as far away as southern Scotland. The earliest church at Rievaulx, of which there are remains in the nave, reflected the austerity of the early Cistercians. As they became more wealthy by sheep rearing, mining and iron-making, lavish extensions were made to their buildings and the abbey church was transformed by a choir built in the finest early Gothic style around 1220. One reason for Rievaulx being unusual is that the abbey was orientated north-south, instead of east-west, in order for the church to fit into the narrow valley of the River Rye. Today there is an excellent audio guide to the abbey as well as a small museum. This contains a selection of abbey artefacts as well as displays of monastery life and information on the extent of the abbey's secular activities.

period of reading and study. This took place in the cloister which was roofed and perhaps glazed.

The arrangement of the monastery buildings around the cloister was almost the same in every Cistercian house, so that it is said that a blind man could find his way round any Cistercian monastery without assistance.

At the side of the cloister is the chapter house where the day-to-day business of the monastery was conducted and where discipline was carried out. Then comes the small parlour where the prior could hold conversations with the brothers, so preserving the silence of the cloister. In one corner of the cloister the warming house, with two huge fireplaces, provided the only source of comfort on a cold winter's day.

Next to the warming house is the impressive refectory and outside the door the remains of the lavatorium where hands were washed before meals. Of the remainder of the buildings at Rievaulx the most impressive is the reredorter, or latrine, standing to its full height above a medieval drain.

Rievaulx Abbey

From the abbey museum, we enter the church and stand in the magnificent monks' choir. Moving on, the transepts show the junction between the earlier work of the original 12th century church and the newer masonry of the choir. The nave was built in a very plain style and only the lower parts of the pillars and walls remain but some idea of the height and style of the church can be gained by looking at the transepts.

The lay brothers worshipped in the nave and a rood screen shut them off from the monks' choir. On the monks' side of the screen was the doorway leading from the church into the cloister, through which the monks passed when they left their early morning worship for a

The monks' infirmary had its own tiny cloister and a splendid hall which by the 15th century had been divided to provide a dignified lodging for the abbot in which he could entertain his noble guests. By the end of the Middle Ages the Cistercian order had become both wealthy and worldly.

St Mary's Church, Rievaulx stands above the Abbey and incorporates the medieval chapel which stood outside the Abbey gateway. It was extended in 1906 by the building of a chancel and bell-tower.

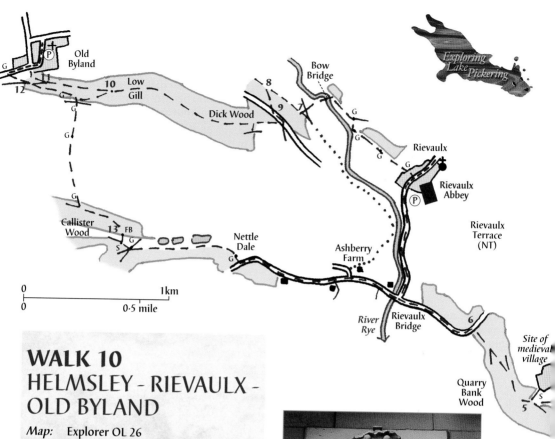

WALK 10
HELMSLEY - RIEVAULX - OLD BYLAND

Map: Explorer OL 26
S.E.P.: Helmsley car park (610838) or
Rievaulx (575849)
Lake Pickering distance: **13.7 miles**

This section of the LPC forms an extra loop up
the Rye valley but is included because of the
area's exceptional historical interest. Possible
variations to the walk include:

(a) a shorter circuit (**4.7 miles**) of
Duncombe Park only

(b) a medium length walk (**10.5 miles**) to
include Duncombe Park and Rievaulx
Abbey

(c) a longer route (**14.0 miles**) which adds
in Old Byland as well.

The medium and longer routes involve an out-
and-back return along part of the same section
of the Cleveland Way. Note that Duncombe Park
is private land and an admission charge should
be expected (£2.00 per adult walker in 2002).
On this occasion I feel the cost is worthwhile
because it gives access to a National Nature
Reserve and a delightful stretch of the River Rye
as well as allowing a circular route, rather than
an out-and-back walk, to be completed.
Permission can be arranged beforehand (01439
770213) or at the Visitor Centre when you start
the walk.

Duncombe Park Circuit

This includes part of the Estate's River Walk and
Country Walk and returns to Helmsley along the
Cleveland Way.

Entering Helmsley on the A170, we follow the
signposts for Duncombe Park and take the
concrete driveway through the parkland. Calling
at the Visitor Centre if necessary, we leave the
driveway by one of the tracks down to the River
Rye – the Estate's River Walk uses the steps at
(1). We then follow the river upstream. More
Geography again! The river has eroded steep
cliffs on the outsides of the meanders while on

Rievaulx Abbey Circuit

Whinny Bank Wood drops away steeply on our left and we soon come to the permissive access route (5) on our right leading up to the deserted medieval village of Griff. It is believed this village was probably cleared and then replaced by a grange near the site of the present Griff Farm.

The path then descends through Quarry Bank Wood (look for wild strawberries in early summer) to reach the road at (6). We turn left, using the roadside path to bring us to the 18th century Rievaulx Bridge. Pausing to admire the gorgeous garden ahead, we then turn right up to the Abbey. We can appreciate the superb setting of the Abbey from the roadside but should, if at all possible, investigate the ruins more fully. An audio guide is available.

the insides there are gently sloping terraces. This section of the river really is a pleasure. We spot the Doric Temple ('Tuscan' on the OS map) through the trees and then come to Mill Bridge. Then as we go up through Park Hill Wood the track becomes concreted again until we reach the top of the rise (2). Now we turn sharp left to leave the River Walk and join the Woodland Walk.

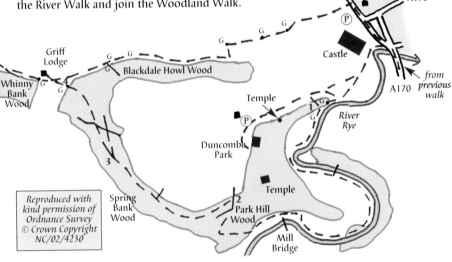

Reproduced with kind permission of Ordnance Survey © Crown Copyright NC/02/4230

At (3) we avoid the works and bear right to the main park driveway where we go left and continue to the estate boundary at (4).

A short distance ahead is Griff Lodge and the Cleveland Way. Those walking the short circuit turn right and follow the clearly marked Cleveland Way back into Helmsley. Those completing either of the two longer walks continue straight ahead on the National Trail.

Continuing along the road, we can visit St Mary's Church before doubling back and taking the path signposted to Bow Bridge. We go through three double gates and then walk on the left of the field boundary, parallel to the line of the old canal which is on the other side of the fence. Waymarks direct us to the delightful old bridge over the Rye. We cross over and then at the path junction (7) we again have a choice of route.

If we are going back to Helmsley (via Ashberry Farm) we turn left; if we are continuing to Old Byland, we stay on the main track which, after a few metres, swings right up the valley side.

Old Byland Circuit

Walking up the slope, we have to turn sharp left at (8) on to the tarmac track and then bear left again at (9) on to the minor road. In a short distance we come to two bridleways on our right. We take the wider of the two, which bends back right down through Dick Wood to the bottom of Mirefalls valley. (Observant ramblers may spot the odd wild garlic or two.)

At (10) we must bear right again and avoid the temptation to go upslope. Horses may have churned up the next part of the path and it can be muddy. It's easy to miss the narrow path going off up to our right at (11) – watch out for a sentinel-like ash tree at the turn-off point. This leads us into Old Byland village. The twelfth-century church merits a visit and there is a 'pay as you drink' facility for walkers who want to refresh themselves with a cuppa.

Making our way back through the village, we take the second bridleway on the left side of the road and descend once more into the dry valley of Mirefalls. At an isolated gate (12) we fork right and then go slightly upslope into the trees.

Leaving the wood, we turn right, cross a farm track and continue south over farmland to Callister Wood. In the trees we bend left and in springtime are again treated to a rich display of woodland flowers, including orchids, before we make our way down to the bottom of Nettle Dale (13).

Using footbridge, stile and gate we follow the acorn symbols of the CW and, once over the stepping stones, turn left on to Bridge Road. Then passing the three ponds on our left, we soon come to tarmac and then carry on to Rievaulx Bridge. From here we retrace our route to Griff Lodge and then continue on the Cleveland Way into Helmsley.

All Saints Church, Old Byland dates from about 1145. Dragons decorate the porch which also has a Saxon sundial on the east face. Little men with rams' horns adorn the chancel arch and the roof beams are from the 15th century.

Special Interest - WALK 10

Duncombe Park

There is a great variety of activities on offer including discovery trails, orienteering courses and a secret garden in addition to the attractions of the House itself and the National Nature Reserve. The video programmes in the visitor centre give an excellent summary of the Duncombe story.

Charles Duncombe bought the Helmsley Estate in 1689 and lived in part of the castle. When he died, the estate passed to his sister and she with her husband built a new home in Duncombe Park. The house was built in 1713 in a fine position overlooking the River Rye but it is perhaps the parkland which is even more interesting. This had been a hunting park for Helmsley Castle long before the mansion was built and deer are still sometimes seen today. A major feature of the landscape planning was the creation of a broad grass terrace following the meander of the River Rye and giving enhanced views down into the valley. At one end of the terrace is a 'ha-ha' – an embankment built behind a retaining wall in order to give an elevated viewpoint. Some believe this to have been one of the first examples of this landscaping device in the country.

Most of the house was destroyed by fire in 1879 but the mansion was rebuilt along the plans of the original building. Following World War I, it was leased to a girls' preparatory school but in 1986 Lord Feversham and his wife moved back into the property and carried out major restoration work.

Nature Reserve

When the park was originally created, much of the woodland was left untouched. It has stayed that way so that today English Nature can claim that here are some of the oldest trees in Europe. There is an invaluable supply of dead and rotting timber which might not at first seem very 'tidy' but it provides ideal habitats for rare fungi and insects. The beetles include the Rievaulx, the spotted longhorn and the black-headed cardinal beetles. Rot holes in the trees provide nest and roost sites for birds and bats which feed on the variety of insects available. In the park are some fine individual trees including what is thought to be, at 44 metres, the country's tallest lime tree and the Woodland Trails give an opportunity for us to discover Old Beauty and the Miracle Tree.

Dan Savage

Rievaulx Abbey

WALK 11
HELMSLEY - POCKLEY

Map: Explorer OL 26
S.E.P.: Helmsley car park (610838)
Lake Pickering distance: **2.1 miles**
Circular walk distance: **9.4 miles**
Special interest: Riccal Dale Woods

If at all possible, this walk should be done in springtime when the bluebells are in flower. Riccal Dale is one of those exquisite locations that, so far, have not yet attracted the attention they deserve.

From the public car park we go to Helmsley market place and then walk in an easterly direction along the A170, turning off left on the side road signed to Carlton and the Youth Hostel. After about 100m we take the path on our right; this is now following Leslie Stanbridge's Whitby Way. We may soon spot some llamas on our right as we continue following the waymarks round field edges and through four gates up to (1). Here we take the left fork of two sets of tractor tracks up to Reagarth Farm and then pass to the right of the main barn, cross over Monk Gardens Lane and carry on by the field edge to Riccal Dale woods.

A little navigational care is now required. We go straight down through the trees to the wide track and turn left. After 25m we avoid the first wide track off to our right but continue for another 60m to a very narrow path, easily missed, on the right. This takes us to the footbridge over the River Riccal (which here may be dry) and then we cross an open piece of land to the main path taking us up into the trees and eventually out of the valley. Then there is a short stretch by the field side before we join the hedged track called Intake Lane which brings us

to the edge of Pockley village. Turning left on the road, we walk to the p.r.o.w. at (2).

Here we may wish to continue a little further to visit Pockley Church. Otherwise we turn left again and admire the view of the Howardian Hills to our left before we take the left-most of three paths at (3) and begin to descend once again into Riccal Dale woods. The next couple of miles are truly delightful. When I first walked the route in May time, I called it 'the blue walk' since there seemed to be blue flowers everywhere: speedwell, forget-me-not, bugle and apparently millions of bluebells!

Crossing the River Riccal at the footbridge (4) we then stay on the main track, recently designated p.r.o.w., as far as the path junction at (5). Here the Link Path crosses our track. We turn sharp left up the steep valley side and follow the Link Path signs through the wood. We bear left at (6) and then continue by the edge of the trees and on a stony track to the road at (7).

Turning left, we can visit Carlton Church and then come back to Keld Lane (8) which leads us across to Ashdale. There is another steep descent to the valley floor where we have to turn abruptly left (9) and take the wide grassy path along the bottom of this dry valley. This is perhaps not as enchanting as Riccal Dale but early spring primroses are certainly attractive.

At (10) we need to be careful to spot the footpath off to our right; it's half-hidden in the trees. (However, if we should miss the turning we will soon come to the road and can turn right and come back into Helmsley that way.) From this point waymarks direct us in a series of zig-zags round field edges and we pass between sports fields to reach Elmslac Road. Going right, then left, we arrive back in Helmsley town centre.

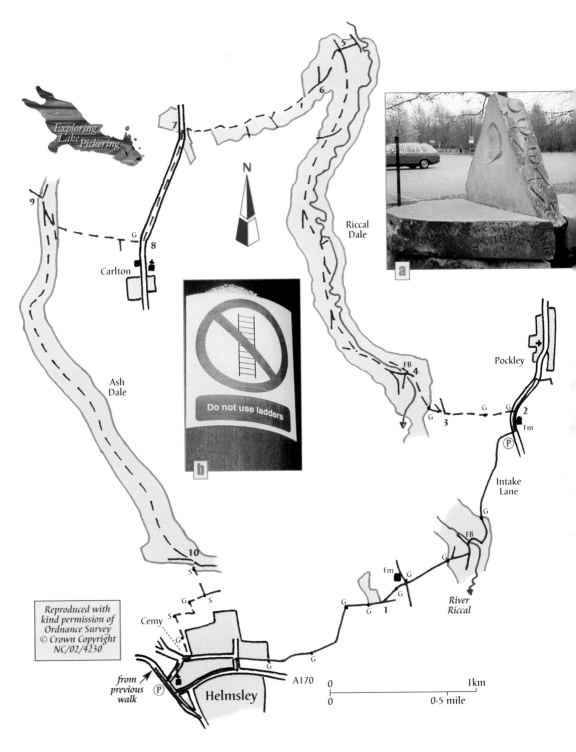

Exploring
Lake Pickering

N

Riccal
Dale

a

Carlton

Ash
Dale

Do not use ladders

b

Pockley

Intake
Lane

River
Riccal

Fm

Reproduced with
kind permission of
Ordnance Survey
© Crown Copyright
NC/02/4230

Cemy

from
previous
walk

Helmsley

A170

0   1km

0   0·5 mile

Special Interest - WALK 11

St John the Baptist's Church, Pockley was built in the 1870s and contains a fine 13th century font. The rood screen was added later and incorporates sculpture from Oberammergau. **St Aidan's Church, Carlton,** built in 1886-87 with its thick walls and small windows gives, according to Pevsner, 'up here on the way to the moor ... a sense of physical and spiritual shelter'. The church may be locked but the unusual exterior is worth seeing.

Special Interest - WALK 12

St Gregory's Minster, Kirkdale is a wonderful church in a wonderful situation. Founded in the 7th century, it was, like Stonegrave (see Walk 5) a minster or centre of Christian mission served by a community of priests. The earlier building fell into ruins in Viking times but crosses built into the outside walls and displayed in the north aisle are from the earlier church.

The church was rebuilt in 1060, shortly before the Norman conquest, as the Saxon sundial above the south doorway records. This tells how Orm, son of Gamel, bought the minster and made it new from the ground. This sundial is the most complete of its kind and bears the longest known Anglo-Saxon inscription.

The west tower, despite its Saxon style, dates from 1827 but the narrow arch between the nave and the tower is Saxon, together with the columns on either side of the chancel arch. The elegant north aisle arcade dates from around 1200. The chancel was rebuilt in 1881.

St Hilda's Church, Beadlam, with its unusual weatherboarding on the bell turret, was built in 1882-3 as a chapel of ease to Kirkdale and contains a huge marble memorial to Lilian Duncombe. 'It is like an Edwardian magazine cover,' comments Pevsner.

St Gregory's Minster

Special Interest - WALK 13

Kirkdale Cave Walking the LPC allows us to let our imaginations run wild thinking of whether the ice melt-water would be too cold for swimming or whether the lake would freeze over enough for skating but as we cross Hodge Beck we should be ready to imagine something perhaps even more bizarre. Kirkdale Cave above the old limestone quarry by Hodge Beck has an amazing story to tell.

In 1821 workmen in the quarry found the remains of numerous animals. When the significance of the discovery was realised, William Buckland made a detailed investigation and after analysis, there were found to be the bones of 22 different species. Some of these included lion, tiger, hippo, rhinoceros and straight-tusked elephant which would only have been able to survive in a warm climate. Others such as the mammoth, woolly rhino and reindeer remains would have been from a cold climate. Clearly, it seemed that the cave had been occupied for an extraordinarily long period and it has been suggested that the remains may date from as far back as c.70,000 BC.

One of the puzzling finds in the cave was the large number of hyena bones. Another surprise was the unusual manner in which the bones of the other creatures had been cracked. So to test his theory that the cave had, in fact, been a hyenas' den William Buckland conducted a cunning experiment. He fed horse, sheep and ox meat to hyenas in two zoos at London and found that the parts of the bones which the living hyenas rejected were the same parts as those which had been left in the cave at Kirkdale. Similarly, the bits of bone which were eaten and digested by the London hyenas were those parts which were absent from the cave remains. Clearly, Buckland concluded, the cave had indeed been a hyenas' den. Balls of solid calcareous droppings were further evidence of occupation by the scavengers.

The thick layer of mud which covered many of the bones in the cave might have been deposited by the waters of Lake Pickering which may have completely submerged the cave.

All Saints Church, Kirkbymoorside, was founded in very early days and is thought to be on the site of a pagan temple. The earliest parts of the present building are Norman. The porch incorporates a priest's chamber on an upper floor. Look for the brass to Lady Brooke (died 1604), the fragment of medieval stained glass, 'the face of God the Father' and a modern window to St Cuthbert. **St Aidan's Church, Gillamoor,** was built in 1802 but includes a screen from 1682 and unusual communion rails from about 1700. The carved stone 'Calvary' over the porch is very unusual.

Special Interest - WALK 14

Kirkbymoorside was the home of George Villiers, whose house we pass as we walk through the town. As a Royalist, he was exiled after the Civil War but then came back and had the courage (or audacity?) to marry the daughter of Lord Halifax, the Parliamentary general who had been rewarded with Villiers' properties. After the Restoration of the Monarchy, however, he received his lands back and became renowned as one of Charles II's favourites, allegedly being as much a loose-liver as his king. He died bankrupt.

St Mary's Church, Lastingham is wonderful: an evocative place with a history going back over 1300 years. Bede tells of the foundation of the church by St Cedd and St Chad around the year 655. Nothing remains of the buildings of the first monastery or of the earliest stone church, except some carved stones exhibited in the crypt and dating from the 8th to 10th centuries.

The Viking invasions of the 9th and 10th centuries evidently brought the Celtic monastery to an end. But after the Norman conquest, Benedictine monks from Whitby came to Lastingham in 1078 and began building a new abbey church. However, before it was finished, the monks left Lastingham in response to a royal invitation to found St Mary's Abbey in York. The unfinished monks' church at Lastingham became the parish church. By 1879 the building was in poor repair and extensive restoration was carried out. Much of the new glass was in memory of the Ringer family who paid for the restoration as a memorial to a 7-year old daughter who had choked to death on a cherry-stone while on holiday in the village. Beneath the east end of the upper church is the unforgettable Norman crypt, itself a miniature aisled church with an east end apse and a stone altar of great antiquity.

Ryedale Folk Museum is advertised as 'not a glass case museum' and includes craft workshops, a fine collection of thatched buildings and an experiment conserving wild cornfield flowers.

Christ Church, Appleton-le-Moors has a spire nearly 30 metres high and a stained glass rose window above the west door. The east end apse (or semicircular recess) has pictures showing the Passion, Death and Resurrection of Jesus.

St Chad's Church, Hutton-le-Hole was erected in 1934 and contains furniture by Robert Thompson, the Kilburn mouseman, and stained glass by the York glass painter, Horace Stammers.

WALK 12
POCKLEY - NAWTON - KIRKDALE

Map: Explorer OL 26
S.E.P.: Pockley (635855) or
A170 lay-by (661849)

Lake Pickering distance:	**4.7 miles**
Circular walk distance:	**9.8 miles**
Shorter walk alternatives:	**4.4 miles;**
	5.4 miles

Special interest:
St Gregory's Minster

This 'circular' walk is more of a figure-of-eight and so can easily be split into two shorter loops if desired. There have been several path diversions, not all clearly indicated in 2002.

We start the walk from Low Farm in Pockley walking towards the village and then taking the first signposted path on our right. After 100m or so we turn right and then follow the field boundary for about 250m to (1) where we turn sharp left. (In 2002 this was not waymarked.) At the end of the field there is a tight squeeze between hedge and fence but then stiles at either end of an open field confirm we are correctly on course. We go up through the trees, turn right to follow the field edge, go right again around Marr Wood, cross over High Lane and then continue along the hedge down to Howldale Lane (2). Turning right once more, this pleasant wooded track leads us down to the A170 and Beadlam Church.

We now go left on the main road for 320m to the path by Huttons Garage (3) which leads us off left to Nawton Primary School. From here the p.r.o.w. passes through a kissing gate and then goes diagonally over a large area of pasture to the gate in the far corner. Then waymarks direct us across more fields to Kirkdale Farm and Guncroft Lane.

On the tarmac we turn left and then right on the track which leads past Lund Head and on to Skiplam Road. Here it's a right turn, then left at the first junction and at the road bend (4) we reach Kirkdale Wood West. Taking the bridleway on our right, it's important not to follow the main track down into the trees but to bear right and keep up just inside the wood. After a short distance the path comes out of the trees but still follows the edge of the wood to a small gate which takes us down to the road. St Gregory's Minster is a little way back to our left; a visit to this gorgeous Saxon church is compulsory!

Once we have finished at St Gregory's we return to the road and, crossing straight over, climb the stile and take the p.r.o.w. which follows the line of Hodge Beck but stays at the top of the steep

river banking. We cross the busy A170, go over a field and then at the next stile cross a driveway and bear slightly right to yet another stile. At the end of the next field (5), however, we ignore the stile and instead turn right and walk to Back Lane.

Climbing over a couple more you-know-whats, our route runs along the field edge to Wombleton. Then after passing the sports ground, a gate leads to a side road; we turn right on to High Street and then right again, going as far as another Back Lane, which is on our left (6). About 30m up on our right we use the stile to cross diagonally over a field to the stile in the opposite corner. There's one more y-k-w and then a clear track, grassy and hedged at first, takes us to the edge of Nawton.

We need to go sharp left at (7) to go past some industrial units and then over two grazing fields to Gale Lane. From here a right turn brings us to the A170.

The next section of the walk is a return (in the opposite direction) up Howldale Lane, down which we came earlier in the day. However, we go past our previous junction (2) and continue on the track to the road at (8). Turning back left on ourselves, we follow the road to the bend at (9) and here turn right on to the wide track.

At the first field boundary we go sharp left through the gap and follow the field edge to Goodhams Dale. Waymarks indicate the diverted route down through the trees and up again to the stile at (10). Going through the hedge, the path brings us out opposite Pockley Church.

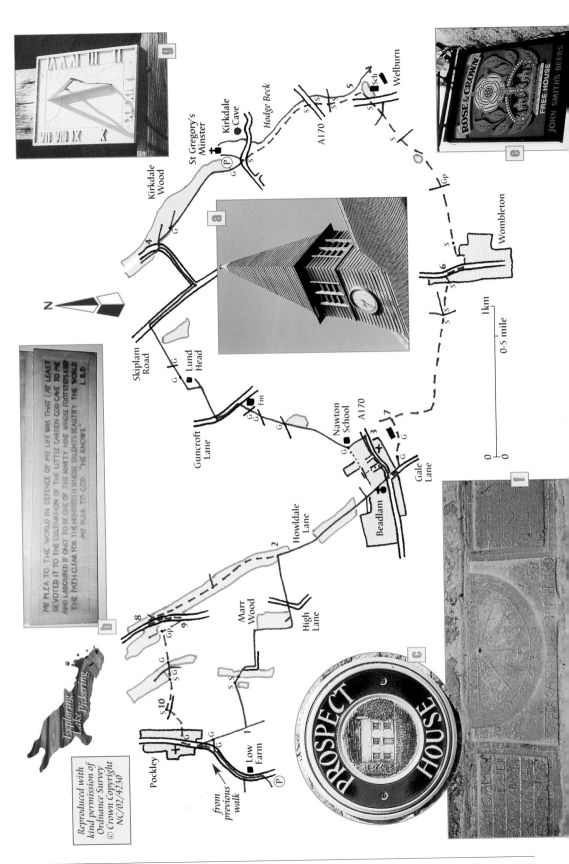

Reproduced with
kind permission of
Ordnance Survey
© Crown Copyright
NC/02/4230

Exploring
Lake Pickering

N

0   0·5 mile   1km

St Gregory's
Minster

Kirkdale
Cave

Hodge Beck

Kirkdale
Wood

Welburn

Sch

A170

Wombleton

Skiplam
Road

Lund
Head

Guncroft
Lane

Fm

Nawton
School

A170

Gale
Lane

Beadlam

Howdale
Lane

Marr
Wood

High
Lane

Pockley

Low
Farm

from
previous
walk

MY PLEA TO THE WORLD IN DEFENCE OF MY LIFE WAS THAT I AT LEAST
DEVOTED IT TO THE CULTIVATION OF THE LITTLE GARDEN GOD GAVE TO ME
AND LABOURED IF ONLY TO BE ONE OF THE NINETY NINE WHOSE FOOTSTEPS KEEP
THE PATH CLEAR FOR THE HUNDREDTH WHOSE TALENTS BEAUTIFY THE WORLD
MY PLEA TO GOD "THE KNOWS"
L.B.D.

ROSE & CROWN
FREE HOUSE
JOHN SMITH'S BEERS

PROSPECT HOUSE

WALK 13
KIRKDALE - KIRKBYMOORSIDE

Map: Explorer OL 26
S.E.P.: St Gregory's Minster (676856)
Lake Pickering distance: **1.7 miles**
Circular walk distance: **9.2 miles**
   (plus 2.2 miles to and from Lowna)
Shorter walk alternative: **4.2 miles**
Special interest:
   Kirkdale Cave

This walk has great variety: a country town, a local nature reserve, a delightful village, a wooded river valley and a world famous cave.

From the car park in the field at the end of the lane to St Gregory's Minster we walk east along the road and over Hodge Beck to the footpath giving access to the famous Kirkdale Cave. It's not sensible to try to climb into the cave, but its historical importance means we should at least say we've seen it.

We carry on to the cross roads at (1) and go through the gate immediately opposite. Going slightly to our left, we pick up the waymarks directing us right along the hedge. When we come to the trees in Robin Hood's Howl (2) we turn sharp right up the slope, cross the stile and continue on the p.r.o.w. into Kirkbymoorside. At first we simply stay by the hedge, but when the path crosses arable land, we may wish to keep to the field edge. Stiles help make the direction clear.

At the houses (3) we veer left and go through the estate. Where the road bends right we branch left and follow the passageway down to the Gillamoor road at (4). Turning right we make our way to High Market Place and go right again into the town centre. A left turn up Church Street takes us to All Saints Church.

As well as looking inside the Church, we may wish to see the Millennium Mosaic Trail next to the churchyard before we continue the walk. We leave the church on the east side next to the Millennium Mosaic Trail and go to the path junction at the edge of the graveyard (4). We take the left, paved fork but note the diversion signs guiding us round the cemetery. Going

through a small gate, the path takes us diagonally over the open field to the corner at (5) and we then go a few metres further to the road. Turning left, then immediately right, we go almost to the end of the road before another left turn leads us to the Manor Vale Nature Reserve. Entering the trees, we pass a remnant of the old castle walls.

At the end of the Nature Reserve (6), the path continues along the right of the field boundary, past the golf course and then bends right to High Park Farm. We go left at the T-junction and then follow the broad track into Gillamoor. This is a delightful village and is worth time exploring. A right turn takes us past the Methodist Chapel and on to St Aidan's Church with its 'Surprise View' of the Dove valley.

(From here, an optional extension of the walk is possible to the Quaker burial ground at Lowna. However, it might be preferable to drive there at the end of the walk.)

Retracing our steps through the village, we continue along Fadmoor Lane to Fadmoor village. Here, turning left at the road junction, then first right, we walk to the stile at (7). A path by the field side now takes us to the minor road at (8) where we go left. Soon at (9) we bear right on the track called Caldron Mill Road and then right again on the very attractive bridleway leading down through Mell Bank Wood.

When we come to the edge of the wood we turn left and follow the course of Hodge Beck as it meanders down Kirk Dale. If we catch glimpses of the river through the trees, we may note how its volume can vary considerably, depending whether or not the water is passing over particularly permeable stretches of limestone rock. Navigation is not a problem; we simply keep to the main track, remembering at Hold Caldron to stay on the left of the river using stile and gate to take the rising path up towards Cat Scar. When we leave Kirkdale Wood, it's only a short way to the footbridge over Hodge Beck and then back to St Gregory's Minster.

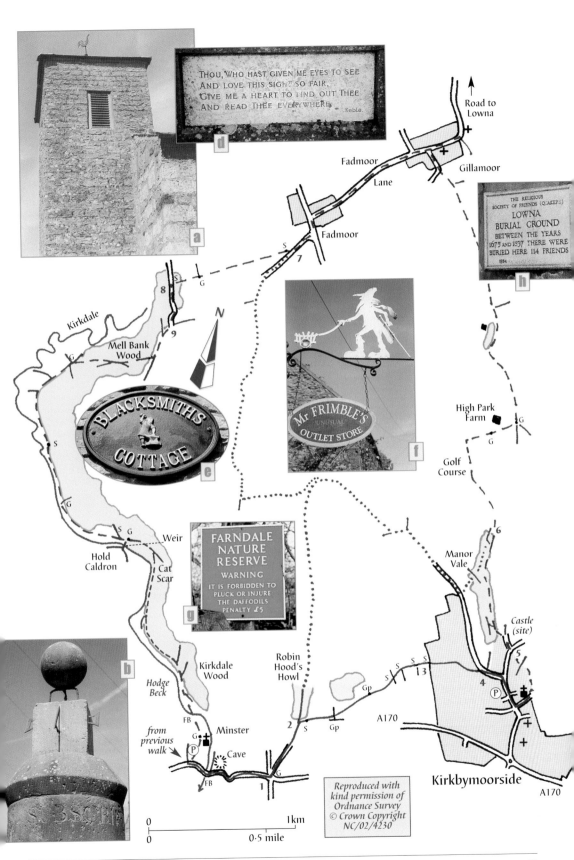

THOU, WHO HAST GIVEN ME EYES TO SEE
AND LOVE THIS SIGHT SO FAIR,
GIVE ME A HEART TO FIND OUT THEE
AND READ THEE EVERYWHERE. — Keble.

d

a

Road to
Lowna

Fadmoor
Lane

Gillamoor

THE RELIGIOUS
SOCIETY OF FRIENDS (QUAKERS)
LOWNA
BURIAL GROUND
BETWEEN THE YEARS
1675 AND 1837 THERE WERE
BURIED HERE 114 FRIENDS
1854

h

Fadmoor

S
7

8
S
S
G

Kirkdale

N

9

Mell Bank
Wood

G

Mr FRIMBLE'S
UNUSUAL
OUTLET STORE

f

High Park
Farm

G

G

BLACKSMITHS
COTTAGE

e

Golf
Course

S

G

G

6

S
G
Weir

Hold
Caldron

Cat
Scar

FARNDALE
NATURE
RESERVE
WARNING
IT IS FORBIDDEN TO
PLUCK OR INJURE
THE DAFFODILS
PENALTY £5

g

Manor
Vale

Castle
(site)

b

Kirkdale
Wood

Robin
Hood's
Howl

Gp

S   S   S
S   1   3

5

4
(P)

Hodge
Beck

2   S   Gp

A170

from
previous
walk

FB

G
(P)   Minster

Cave

FB

1

G

Reproduced with
kind permission of
Ordnance Survey
© Crown Copyright
NC/02/4230

Kirkbymoorside

(P)

+

+

A170

S.J. B.SC.II.

0   1km

0   0·5 mile

WALK 14
KIRKBYMOORSIDE – APPLETON-LE-MOORS

Map: Explorer OL 26
S.E.P.: Kirkbymoorside car park (696866) or
         Appleton-le-Moors (735881)
Lake Pickering distance: **3.4 miles**
Circular walk distance: **10.7 miles**
Shorter walk alternatives: **8.6 miles;**
                            5.5 miles

Special interest:
   Kirkbymoorside, Lastingham,
   Ryedale Folk Museum

Navigation from here on is much easier. Turning left, we follow the wide track to (10) where we join the Link Path and, turning right, walk along South Ings Lane to Appleton-le-Moors. We should look inside Christ Church with its unusual apse before continuing NNW to Hamley Lane (11). Turning right, we now follow this quiet road as far as the stile at (12).

This walk includes farmland, a little woodland, a limestone quarry and a touch of heather moor as well as the major pilgrimage centre of Lastingham.

From Kirkbymoorside car park we turn right down the main road and then left along Howe End. We bend right on Old Road and then left along Swineherd Lane to the footpath at (2). This takes us through half-a-dozen kissing gates to the road at (3); it's almost all pasture, though the last field is arable land.

Turning left on the road, past the site of the former Keldholme Priory (nothing remains today), then left at the T-junction, we branch off right on the path at (4). This leads over farmland to the stile at (5). The path over the next section may not be too clear. We have to bear down diagonally right through scrub and bracken and then through a thicket of hawthorns to the footbridge over Hutton Beck. Then crossing over the quarry road, we take the *centre* of the three tracks (6). (This is not the p.r.o.w. shown on the O.S map.) We then follow the waymarks round to the slope at (7).

Going up the side of the reclaimed slope, we cross two stiles as we enter a small wood. Again the path might be a little overgrown, so leggings may be sensible. Then at (8) the path comes to a dead end as we face an impenetrable barrier of trees blocking the way. Here the p.r.o.w. (no waymark visible) leaves the trees and cuts diagonally right over ploughland to the field corner stile on Headlands Road (9).

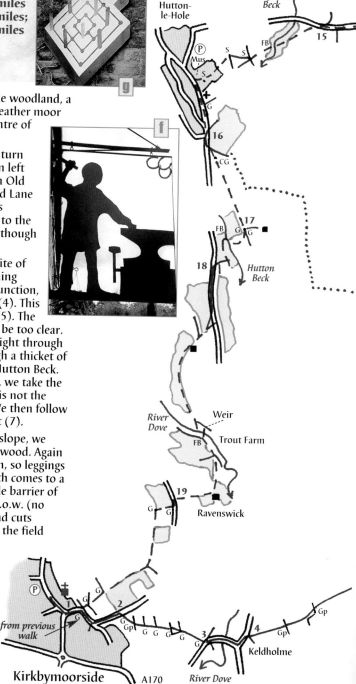

This takes us to the path running along the right-hand side of Hagg Wood and then through trees beside Ings Beck. We soon go right over a delightful footbridge and are guided by waymarks into Lastingham.

However long we decide to spend exploring the village we should, at the very

least, investigate St Mary's Church and its historic crypt. Then afterwards as we walk on, we bear right on the track at (13). This brings us to the edge of the heather moor and at the gate we turn left on to the path running by the boundary wall.

At (14) we go right on the road, then at (15) branch off left on the grassy track. Soon after another footbridge, the p.r.o.w. splits into two. If we take the right fork, we will come out on the road immediately next to the Ryedale Folk Museum.

Our route now turns left and we soon reach St Mark's Church before carrying on to the path junction at (16). Here we bear slightly left into Oxclose Lane and then walk as far as the two gates at (17). We go through the gate on our *right* immediately before the gate across the road in front of us. Walking down the slope, we bend round the clump of trees to our right and reach the gated footbridge over Hutton Beck. From here the path takes us up to the road (18).

Turning left and using the wide grass verge, we go to the stony track signposted to Douthwaite Dale. Avoiding any side-turns, we walk downhill to yet another footbridge, this time over the River Dove. Crossing the river, we pass the trout farm and head up past Ravenswick to join Swineherd Lane (19). A left-right turn puts us back on the footpath and waymarks then send us along field edges back to Kirkbymoorside, though we need to note the warning not to feed the horses; they may bite!

Reproduced with kind permission of Ordnance Survey © Crown Copyright NC/02/4230

0 ————— 1km
0 ————— 0·5 mile

WALK 15
APPLETON-LE-MOORS
- WRELTON

Maps: Explorer OL 26 & Explorer OL 27
S.E.P.: Appleton-le-Moors (735879) or
Wrelton (767861)
Lake Pickering distance: 3.8 miles
Circular walk distance: 10.5 miles
Shorter walk alternatives: 6.3 miles;
7.8 miles

Special interest:
Beadale Wood, Cropton Brewery

On this walk we pass through four villages and have the opportunity to visit the Roman Camps at Cawthorn, though it is probably preferable to make this the focus of the next walk.

Parking in Appleton-le-Moors, we walk SSE down the main street from Christ Church and at the road corner (1) continue straight on down the bridleway to (2). Here the p.r.o.w. splits into two; we take the waymarked one which forks right, crosses a field and then enters Bishop Hagg Wood. This is the first of several wooded sections we follow on this walk. The path is firm, then widens out as 'The Stripe' track as we continue along the River Seven and enter Sinnington.

Crossing the road bridge (1767) over the Seven we call at the Methodist Church just to our right before doubling back and returning through the village following signs for 'The (New) Hall' and 'The (Anglican) Church'. The route goes round the side of the church and takes the grassy footpath going roughly ENE. There's a diversion at (3) to the other side of the hedge and then we pass alongside a recently planted wood – 'one of 200 new community woods created by the Woodland Trust to mark the 2000 millennium'.

There's another slight diversion at (4) over the ancient Double Dike and then after crossing a ditch we make for the gate at (5). Going through, we bear left and continue alongside pasture keeping the tall hedge immediately to our left.

We cross the road by Coppice Farm and then carry on over four more stiles into Wrelton. We can bypass the village by using the path at (6) but it's worth walking through the village if only to spot the site of the old vineyard at Vinery Farm. Then at the road bend (7) just after the Wesley Chapel we turn back left on to a path and then at the second stile go right and soon enter Beadale Wood (8).

Where the path divides (9) we must hop over the broken-down wall and bear right to continue on the p.r.o.w. This may be a bit overgrown in summer but the line of the path is still obvious. Then at the path crossing (10) we turn right but a little further on (11) there may be some

confusion. Soon after emerging from the trees, we *ignore* the waymarked bridleway going right but instead continue straight ahead along the field edge on the other, diverted, bridleway which is not waymarked. Reaching Straights Lane (12) the route is clearer. We turn left and follow the track north, bending left through the gate (13), then going on to High Lane.

At this point there is the option of visiting the Roman Camps, just to our right. Otherwise we go left on the road for a mile or so and then left again at the path entrance to Whitethorn caravan site (14). After 100m we climb over a stile and here we are requested to follow yet another diversion; instead of going diagonally across the field we walk round two sides of the field to the gate at the far corner (15). The path carries on to the road and then we go left into Cropton.

At the sign for the Link Path (16) we branch off right to look at St Gregory's Church. On leaving we go straight to the main road and turn right, right again and left through the village to the New Inn with its brewery and Visitor Centre. But immediately before the pub, we turn right along the path which leads us down to rejoin the Link route bridleway at (17).

We go left along Low Lane, a delightful track leading through trees to the path junction at (18). Remaining on the Link route, we bend right here, cross the River Seven again and then continue on the Link as far as (19). Now we must be careful. It's very easy to miss our turning. We go left off the tarmac on to a wide track and walk for just 25m to a half-hidden path on our right. This takes us up through the trees and then we walk along the field edge back into Appleton-le-Moors.

Special Interest - WALK 15

All Saints Church, Sinnington was restored in 1904 but two Norman doorways were retained as well as pre-conquest stones built into the church walls. The communion rail and some benches are from the 17th century. **St Gregory's Church, Cropton** with its imitation Norman doorway, dates from 1844. The stump of the Cropton Cross remains. **Cropton Brewery** opened in 1984 in the cellars of the village pub. Visiting groups are welcome.

Beadale Wood – This Ancient Semi-Natural Woodland (at least 400 years old) is being restored to its former coppiced nature. Coppicing allows light to penetrate to the woodland floor and so encourages a wider variety of plants but also the regular cutting of the trees is allowing a small charcoal producing industry to develop. Apparently all native British hardwood trees respond well to coppicing and repeated cutting back increases the life of a tree.

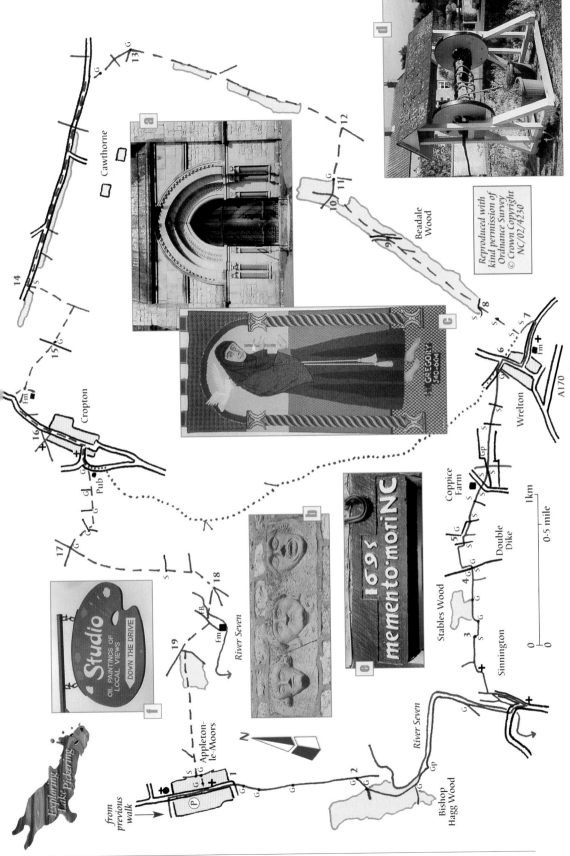

Exploring Late Pickering

from previous walk →

Appleton-le-Moors

Studio
OIL PAINTINGS OF
LOCAL VIEWS
DOWN THE DRIVE

f

N

River Seven

b

1695
memento·moriNC

e

River Seven

Bishop
Hagg Wood

Sinnington

Stables Wood

Double
Dike

Coppice
Farm

Wrelton

A170

Beadale
Wood

ST GREGORY
540-604

c

a

Cawthorne

Cropton

Pub

d

Reproduced with
kind permission of
Ordnance Survey
© Crown Copyright
NC/02/4230

0   0.5 mile
0   1km

WALK 16
WRELTON - PICKERING

Map: Explorer OL 27
S.E.P.: Wrelton (767861) or
         Pickering car park (796840)
Lake Pickering distance: **3.2 miles**
Circular walk distance: **10.1 miles**
  (plus 2.0 miles round Roman camps)
Shorter walk alternative: **5.7 miles**
Special interest: Cawthorn Roman Camps

Notes:

(1) The firing range in Pickering Woods is in use
on Sundays from April to October and the full
circuit cannot be walked on these days.

(2) The N.Y.M. National Park produces a helpful
guide to the Roman Camps and it may be
useful to obtain this before setting off on the
walk.

(3) Although it is possible to walk on quiet roads
and paths south of the A170, the LPC route
from Wrelton to Pickering follows a more
interesting line along the main road. There is a
roadside footpath all the way and this route
allows us to visit Middleton Church and view
Middleton's interesting architecture.

Starting in Wrelton from wherever we
left off on Walk 15, we take the minor
road out of the village, join the A170 and
then walk through Aislaby. We
carry on to Middleton to visit
the church and then continue to
the side road (1) which takes us
into Pickering. (At Crook Lane, a
short walk turns left, though this
will mean missing the link on the LPC
between here and Pickering.)

We walk to Beck Isle Museum but take the
signposted track on our left immediately before
the museum (2). This soon becomes a narrower
path but we keep following the directions round
to (3). At this point we avoid the path going on
ahead but veer diagonally right across pasture to
a gate. From here the path continues parallel to
the railway to (4) where we have to turn right,
cross the railway and then go left on the road.
We are now leaving the main LPC route.

Crossing over New Bridge, we quickly branch
left into the RMC Aggregates quarry driveway.
Then where the track forks, we bear right to the
'Concrete Plant' and then slightly right again to
the gate at (5). This leads into Pickering Woods
(note the restriction mentioned above) and the
peaceful environment makes a sharp contrast
with the quarry we've just left. We follow the
track to (6); ignore the branch left but go
straight ahead and then, just behind the brick

wall target area, take the left of the two tracks
rising in front of us. The stretch through Haugh
Wood is very enjoyable and has the distinction
of lying on the top of the ridge rather than, as
with many of the wooded walks in this area,
being along the valley floor.

Leaving the wood, we cross one field, go along
the edge of another and then follow the Haugh
Rigg track to the path turn-off at (7). We
observe the directions guiding us by the field-
side, then turn right down into Saintoft Slack
and then left to Saintoft Grange.

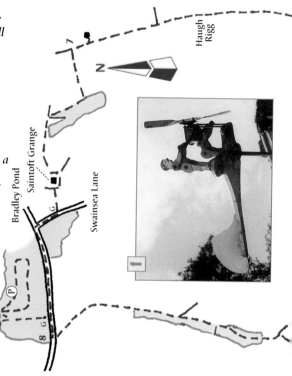

The p.r.o.w. goes round the farm and then at
Swainsea Lane we turn right to Bradley Road.
Here we go left and walk to the entrance to the
Cawthorn Roman Camps.

The National Park's guided trail is about a mile
long and is definitely worth following. Then
when we've finished our investigation, we go
back to Bradley Road, turn right and walk for
about 150m to (8). From here we more or less
follow, in reverse, the route used on the
previous walk. We go roughly south as far as (9)
but instead of turning right at this point, carry
on along Straights Lane to the track T-junction
at (10) and here turn right and follow the
signed route across to Beadale Wood. At the
edge of the trees, the path forks and either route
will take us down to the main track on the valley
floor where we turn left back to Wrelton.

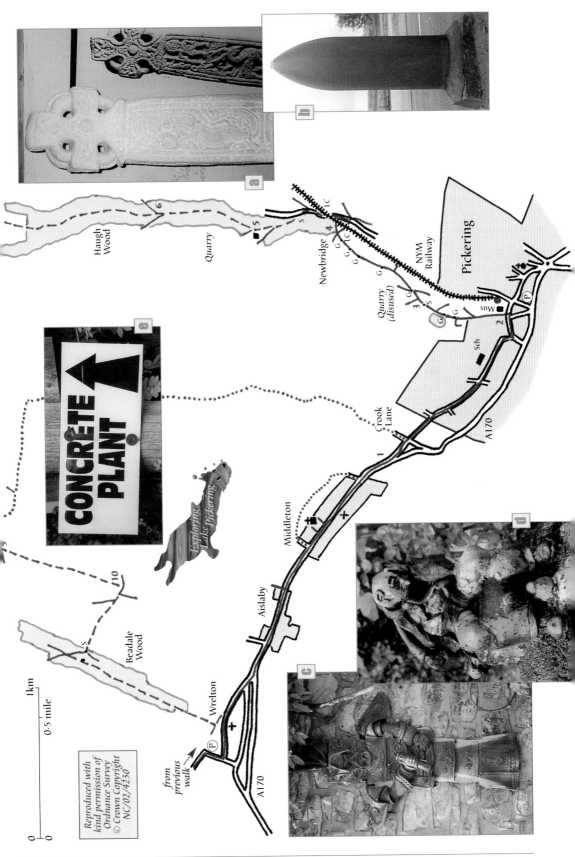

Haugh Wood

Quarry

6

S 5

Newbridge

S

4 LC

G
G
G

Quarry (disused)

G
G

3 S
G
G
G

NYM Railway

Pickering

2

Mus

P

Sch

Crook Lane

A170

1

Middleton

Aislaby

Wrelton

Beadale Wood

S

J10

Exploring Little Pickering

CONCRETE PLANT

from previous walk

P

A170

Reproduced with kind permission of Ordnance Survey © Crown Copyright NC/02/4230

1km

0·5 mile

0
0

Special Interest - WALK 16

Cawthorn Roman Camps

Although there is no evidence of Roman buildings, the area of the forts has been cleared and the layout of the camps can easily be seen. Wheelchairs can be used on the marked trail which is about a mile long. What is particularly interesting about the Cawthorn Camps is that there are three different structures and, almost inevitably, archaeologists have had different opinions concerning their use. The basic question has been whether they were practice training camps or permanent forts.

The guided trail leads us first to what is believed to have been a **marching camp.** One Roman military writer said that the Roman army carried a walled town with them wherever they marched. He was referring to the fact that at the end of a day's march in hostile territory the Roman army would construct a temporary camp with protective bank, ditch and wooden stockade. As we survey the size of the structure today, we cannot help but be impressed with the efficiency of Roman military organisation. We can still see the gateways to the camp, with their strategically curved defensive ramparts ('claviculae'). These were designed so that attacking Britons could reach the entrance from one side only and right-handed men had the severe disadvantage of not being able to hold their shields in their right hands.

We move on to the **first fort** and realise that this was a more substantial construction than the marching camp. As all three gates from the camp are on the side next to the fort, it has been suggested that the camp could have been used as a base while the bigger fort was being erected. At some later stage, this fort was enlarged with the addition of an extra annexe to the east. There is a well-worn path around the perimeter of the fort but we are requested not to use this in order to restrict erosion of the monument. Instead we are directed on the trail path round to the second, more significant fort.

We enter the **second fort** on a causeway built up across the defensive ditches and go through one of the gateways located in the centre of the fort's walls. Usually there were four gates, one for each wall, but in this case the northern wall lies next to a steep cliff and a gate was presumably unnecessary. Attackers must have been extremely brave (or foolhardy) to mount an assault on a Roman fort. They had to cross the 'ankle breaker' channels and two Punic ditches and then faced a high palisaded rampart. What made the ditches particularly nasty was their asymmetric profile; it was easy to jump into the ditch but far harder to escape out of it because of the steeply sloping back wall.

It seems likely that this was the last of the works to be constructed because it cuts into the side of the marching camp; perhaps the other fort had been a practice exercise before the 'real' one was constructed. Before we leave the fort, we must go to the viewing point in the north wall; the magnificent vista from the top of the precipitous Tabular Hills scarp shows why the Romans chose this strategic location to build their fortifications. Cawthorn may have been abandoned when Hadrian was building his northern frontier wall in the 120s and it was felt that this part of England was sufficiently pacified to allow the Roman garrisons to be removed.

When we return to the car park, we have the option of a short stroll through the woods which have grown here since World War II as a result of the cessation of grazing and heather burning on this part of the moors.

St Andrew's Church, Middleton has an Anglo-Saxon tower and Norman arcades. There are four 15th century choir stalls, one with an interesting misericord, and an 18th century pulpit. The chief glory of the church is the collection of five pre-conquest crosses displayed in the north aisle. Look for the hunter with his scramasax and the dragon-like Jellinge animal.

Special Interest - WALK 17

Pickering Castle

Pickering's first castle was built around 1069-70 to help William the Conqueror keep control of this area following the revolts by northerners against the French occupation. The castle was the motte-and-bailey type on a raised mound with timber fortifications. On the other side of the valley of Pickering Beck stands Beacon Hill, another castle mound, and this may be the site of a siegework erected in the 12th or 13th century for attacking the castle.

Various repairs and improvements were made to the castle and especially important was the gradual replacement of wood by stone, less liable to rot and not susceptible to fire. However, the outer defences of the castle remained in wood until the early 14th century and records remain telling us how many oak trees were being cut for repair and maintenance work.

For a short time after 1267 the castle and Honour (i.e., the area controlled by the feudal landlord) were given to Edmund Crouchback, Earl of Lancaster but when his son Thomas rebelled against the King in 1321, the crown immediately seized all Lancastrian lands, including Pickering.

Pickering Castle

Then in 1322 after Pickering had been spared from Robert the Bruce and his invading Scots army, Edward II made considerable improvements to the castle including the building of a stone curtain wall and three stone towers. However, with Edward's death (1327) the castle returned to the Lancastrians.

During the 15th and 16th centuries the castle seems to have declined and its demise was hastened when Sir Richard Chomley removed 13 wagonloads of stone and two loads of slate to help build his own new house at Roxby two miles away.

Although occupied by Cromwell's forces, Pickering Castle, unlike Helmsley, played no active part in the Civil War (1642-50) and its useful life by this time was finished.

St Peter and St Paul Church, Pickering contains an outstanding collection of medieval wall paintings which give a vivid idea of what many churches looked like in the Middle Ages. The arcades in the church date from the 12th century and above them are the mid-15th century paintings. On the north side there are saints: George with a surprised looking dragon,

Christopher with some very odd fish, Edmund killed by twenty arrows and John the Baptist beheaded. On the south side St Catherine is shown suffering martyrdom. Then come the seven acts of mercy (from Jesus' parable of the sheep and the goats in Matthew 25) and scenes from Christ's passion and resurrection. There is an elegant 18th century pulpit and a fine triple sedilia (clergy seats) in the chancel.

All Saints, Thornton-le-Dale is a 14th century church restored and partially rebuilt in 1866. A recumbent figure (modelled on Lady Beatrice Hastings?) lies in the sanctuary.

WALK 17
PICKERING –
THORNTON-LE-DALE –
ELLERBURN

Map: Explorer OL 27
S.E.P.: Pickering car park (796840)
Lake Pickering distance: **4.7 miles**
Circular walk distance: **9.1 miles**
Shorter walk alternatives: **7.0 miles;**
                             5.5 miles

Special interest:
 Pickering Castle and Church, Newtondale,
 N.Y.M. Railway

This walk offers the chance to explore Pickering as well as to visit Thornton-le-Dale. The last section of the walk comes down the Newtondale gorge along which the glacial meltwaters poured and through which the N.Y.M. Railway runs today.

The walk starts from the car park opposite the T.I.C.. Turning right out of the car park, then right again along Market Place, we go ESE towards the Parish Church with its medieval wall paintings. From here we go down to the main road roundabout and left up Kirkham Lane to Ruffa Lane (1).

We follow Ruffa Lane through the houses and then continue along the track and then the field- edge path to the gap in the fence at (2). Here the short circuit walk turns left; the longer walk goes right on the path up through the trees and then we make for Hagg House. There's been a minor path diversion but, crossing the farm drive, we take the stile into the trees opposite. Waymarks lead us to the stile in the hedge at (3). From here we have to cross four fields. We may want to avoid standing crops by going round field edges but the p.r.o.w. goes across the fields. Navigation is helped by aiming for the stiles and we eventually reach the A170 road at (4).

Walking into Thornton-le-Dale we continue through the village on the main road and then turn off left on the path alongside Thornton Beck. At Priestman's Lane a right turn and a short diversion allows us to visit All Saints' Church. Then coming out of the church, we return down Priestman's Lane and follow the stream to the former Thornton Mill, now modernised into the offices of a pet foods manufacturer. The path skirts the mill and follows the beck round to Low Farm.

At the farm we go left to St Hilda's Church, Ellerburn, and from the church we take the footpath northwards along Kirkdale Slack – if it's early September be careful not to trip over the scores of pheasants on the track. Then we carry on through the trees to the path junction at (5).

Turning left, we join the Low Dalby Forest road and here turn left again, and then after about 300m, left once more (6), following the tarmac round to the track on our right at (7). Taking this, we soon branch left (8) on to the signposted track. We descend through trees into Howl Dale, going left at the path T-junction and then soon turning sharp right at the waymark (9). (The path continuing down Howl Dale is the short circuit route.)

Ascending and following the edge of two fields, then walking just inside Scalla Moor Plantation, we soon cross the A169 Whitby Road and continue towards Newtondale.

Shortly after entering Little Park Wood, we have a choice of several routes down Newtondale into Pickering. My preference is to use the valley bottom route beside Pickering Beck. For this we take the path down the steep valley side and, after ignoring two earlier cross-tracks, turn right (10) at the path T-junction. We need to be careful not to miss the narrow path 10m further on leading off to our left and taking us down to the footbridge over the beck.

However, immediately before the bridge, we take the path going left and we follow the tightly meandering stream down valley. When we leave the trees at (11) we enter an Open Access area. The best line to follow is probably straight down the meadowland, following tractor lines and keeping close to the stream on our right. However, when we come to the stile at (12) we can cross the fence and use the path inside the trees and then continue to the road at (13).

Turning left, we take the path upwards immediately on our left. This runs parallel to the road but away from the traffic, past a line of disused quarries, before re-joining the road on the outskirts of Pickering. From here, we carry straight on into the town, branching left at (14) if we are visiting the castle.

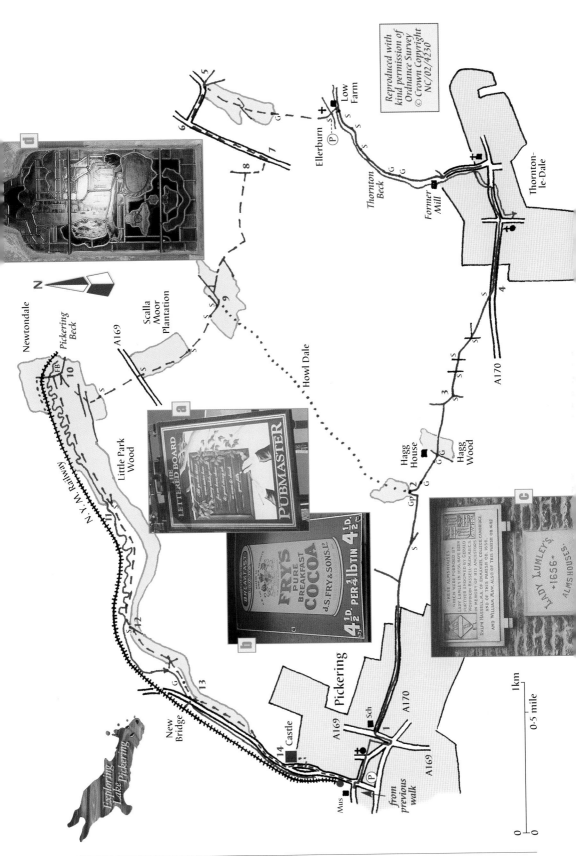

Reproduced with
kind permission of
Ordnance Survey
© Crown Copyright
NC/02/4230

Newtondale

Pickering Beck

A169

Scalla Moor Plantation

Thornton Beck

Ellerburn

Low Farm

Thornton-le-Dale

Former Mill

Howl Dale

Hagg House

Hagg Wood

A170

N.Y.M. Railway

Little Park Wood

Exploring Lake Pickering

New Bridge

Castle

Pickering

Sch

A169

A170

A169

Mus

from previous walk

THE LETTERED BOARD
PUBMASTER

FRY'S PURE BREAKFAST COCOA
J.S.FRY & SONS.LD.

LADY LUMLEY'S
1656
ALMSHOUSES

0.5 mile

1km

WALK 18
ELLERBURN - GIVENDALE

Map: Explorer OL 27
S.E.P.:   Ellerburn Church (841842) or
           Dalby Forest (856876)
Lake Pickering distance: **3.3 miles**
Circular walk distance: **10.5 miles**
Shorter walk alternative: **4.8 miles**
Special interest: Dalby Forest Visitor Centre

Ellerburn Church has a small private car park. The vicar is willing to allow walkers visiting the church and doing the LPC to park here; a donation in the gift box inside church would be appreciated. There is a great variety of possible trails through Dalby forest - the one suggested here has a good surface and is easy to follow.

Taking the tarred track eastwards from Ellerburn Church, we bend right to pass the Welham Park Trout Farm on our left at Low Paper Mill Farm. We then go through a gate to the unmarked and not very clear bridleway at (1) where we branch right over pasture, aiming diagonally for the gate in the opposite field corner. From this gate the track becomes clearer and, after keeping right at the track fork, we continue through three more gates out on to the track crossing at (2).

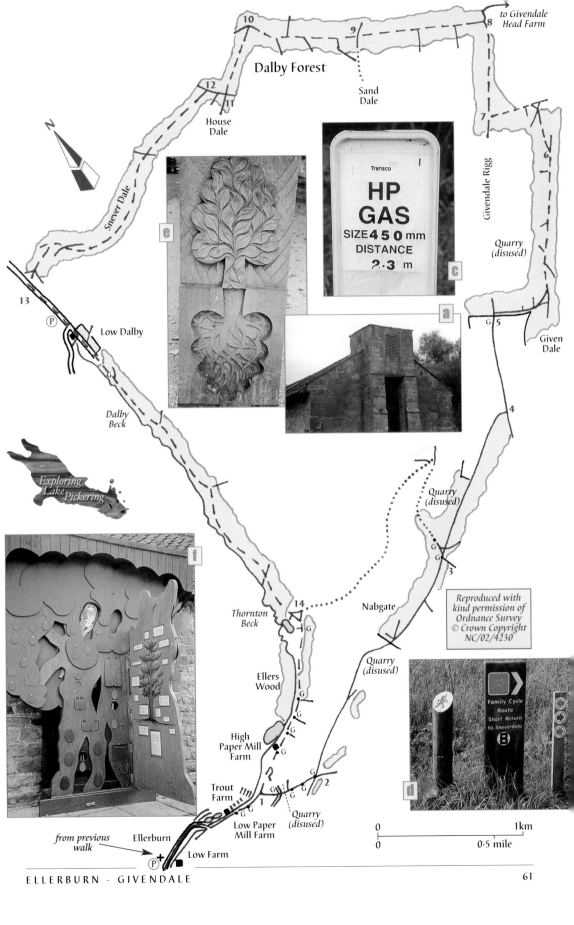

to Givendale
Head Farm

10

9

8

Dalby Forest

Sand
Dale

12

11

House
Dale

Givendale Rigg

7

6

Sneyer Dale

N

e

Transco

**HP
GAS**

SIZE **450** mm
DISTANCE
2·3 m

c

Quarry
(disused)

13

a

P

Low Dalby

G 5

Given
Dale

Dalby
Beck

4

Exploring
Lake Pickering

Quarry
(disused)

G
G

3

f

14

Nabgate

Thornton
Beck

G

Reproduced with
kind permission of
Ordnance Survey
© Crown Copyright
NC/02/4230

Ellers
Wood

G

Quarry
(disused)

G

High
Paper Mill
Farm

G

G

Family Cycle
Route
Short Return
to Sneverdale

E

d

Trout
Farm

G

G

2

1

G

0   1km

0   0·5 mile

from previous
walk

Ellerburn

Low Paper
Mill Farm

Quarry
(disused)

P

Low Farm

From here the route is obvious. We turn left on to the main track and after reaching the trees at Nabgate we soon enter the Forest Enterprise property at (3). Those opting for the short walk turn left here, go down the valley side into Sand Dale and then turn left back to Ellerburn. The other walks continue straight on, going through the gorse, heather and bracken which here accompany the birch and conifers.

After emerging from the trees and then following a field edge path, we round the corner of the wood and come to a T-junction (4). We turn left on a wide track to the gate at the edge of the trees (5) and here we turn immediately right on the narrow path down into the bottom of Given Dale. On the floor of the valley is a broad forest drive; we turn left and walk up the gentle slope.

Where the track bends and forks (6) we keep left, remaining on the forest drive, and then a little while later we swing more sharply left and continue round for another 350m to the junction at (7). We are now on Given Dale Rigg. A right turn takes us to (8) and there we turn sharp left.

At the third forest ride on our left (9), we can turn down Sand Dale on another broad grit and gravel trail which will join with the short walk two miles downvalley at (15). However, if we are doing the full walk, we carry on half a mile for another four forest rides as far as the bend at (10). Here is the tarred road leading down into

House Dale and thence to Low Dalby settlement. We follow this road for nearly 500m to the first main track crossing (11). We go right to the second track on our left (12) and then take this route which leads us on a good firm earth surface down Snever Dale. When we come to the picnic site (13), we turn left on the road to Low Dalby.

At Low Dalby there is the opportunity to browse round the Visitor Centre with its various displays of forest management. We then continue due south at the edge of the forest, first alongside Dalby Beck and then beside Thornton Beck. When we come to (14) we can spend a few minutes going down to the hide at Ellerburn Pond before continuing on the path along Thornton Beck, past the High and Low Paper Mill Farms and back to our starting point.

Special Interest – WALK 18

Dalby (The Great Yorkshire Forest) Visitor Centre has a variety of fascinating displays and badger watches, owl hunts, and fungus forages are all part of the annual events programme.

St Hilda's Church, Ellerburn is a hidden gem in a secluded valley. It was built before the Normans came but has been much changed down the centuries. There are numerous carved stones set in the south and east walls and intriguing carving on the chancel arch.

Exploring Lake Pickering – supporting Christian Aid

Set up in the mid forties, Christian Aid works in the less developed countries of Asia, Africa and Latin America, combating poverty and injustice and seeking to put into practice Christian teaching about human dignity and the equal worth of all people. It believes that the poor and powerless should be given, or given back, the means to help themselves. This is the most effective and respectful way of helping them to improve their lives.

Christian Aid and the other development agencies often combine resources to support particular projects overseas and they cooperate with each other so that there is a sharing of information and expertise. Christian Aid does not have permanent staff overseas or projects of its own. It concentrates maximum resources on help for long-term projects that tackle the causes of poverty.

There is another side to Christian Aid, one which is seen at times of sudden crisis. When a major disaster such as the current African famine occurs, Christian Aid joins with other British development agencies which make up the Disasters Emergency Committee and a joint appeal is launched via the media. This co-ordinates the relief effort and helps to avoid unnecessary duplication.

For more details about Christian Aid please write to:
Christian Aid, PO Box 100, London SE1 7RT
www.christian-aid.org.uk

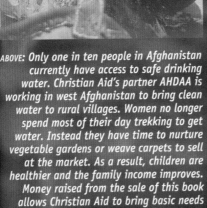

ABOVE: Only one in ten people in Afghanistan currently have access to safe drinking water. Christian Aid's partner AHDAA is working in west Afghanistan to bring clean water to rural villages. Women no longer spend most of their day trekking to get water. Instead they have time to nurture vegetable gardens or weave carpets to sell at the market. As a result, children are healthier and the family income improves. Money raised from the sale of this book allows Christian Aid to bring basic needs like water within people's reach.

WALK 19
GIVENDALE - ALLERSTON - EBBERSTON

Map: Explorer OL 27
S.E.P.: Allerston (878829) or
Ebberston (899827)
Lake Pickering distance: **4.0 miles**
Circular walk distance: **9.8 miles**
Shorter walk alternatives: **7.0 miles;**
4.8 miles

Special interest:
Ebberston Hall, Chafer Wood

The joining point on the LPC between Walks 18 and 19 lies halfway down Given Dale, so we take up the LPC route in Allerston village where there is some limited parking space and go east to Ebberston. This means that we do the Given Dale LPC section at the end of the circular walk.

From Allerston Parish Church we take the main road through the village, past the old mill and the Methodist Chapel, to the path on our left squeezed between gardens. We follow this back to the path turn-off at (1). This takes us along a hedged path and then at the fourth gap/gate (2) we locate a small gate on our left which leads us across arable land. We follow the boundary of a very large field, crossing Bloody Beck at (3). Then going through the second kissing-gate (not the big gate) we cross the stream again (4) and veer diagonally over the field to the opposite corner. Here we go straight across the tarred track, follow the beck through the trees, then cross rough grazing and bear right to join the road at (5).

Turning left, we go up through Ebberston village, past the Methodist Chapel, to the A170. To visit Ebberston Church and Ebberston Hall requires an out-and-back detour along the A170; some may prefer to do that now but assuming we leave that treat to the end of the walk, we cross straight over the main road and walk to the Chafer Wood Nature Reserve notice board (6). Here we turn left, go past the recently repaired old pinfold, follow the path uphill and go round to the shelter built as King Alfred's Cairn. The views over the 'Lake' from this vantage point are superb.

We continue north on the p.r.o.w. just within the wood and then at (7) make use of the concessionary path which goes off right before soon turning northwards again. This is a very attractive route, cut through the bracken and brambles and

with some newly planted trees. Eventually the way ahead is blocked by a stiled fence so we turn right and descend to a wider track at the bottom of Netherby Dale where we go left and shortly reach the road (8).

Going left, a short stretch of tarmac leads to the bridleway marked 'Private Road'. Here the short circuit bears off left but the long walk uses the private road to Malton Cote. Just before the caravan site, we go left over the waymarked stile. The next half-mile or so is exceptional because we walk along the ancient earthworks overlooking Scamridge Slack. When we come to the trees at (9) the path has been diverted so that we walk round the enclosure but as we do so we see in the trees well-preserved remains of the Scamridge Dykes.

Turning left on to the bridleway, the route follows a broken limestone wall and then joins the Link Path (10) running by the side of Lingy Plantation. We go left again along a wide earth-grass track (muddy in season) to the road at (11). Now we go right, over more ancient dikes and soon reach Givendale Head Farm. We go left round the back of the farm to the finger-post just past the end of the buildings (12).

From here we turn left, walking roughly southwards, past the former farm pond and then bending left to follow the p.r.o.w. which runs through pasture down the bottom of the dry valley or 'slack'. The stile at the entrance to the forest may be overgrown but once this is negotiated our way is clear. We take the muddy path straight ahead, or go right-left if we prefer, and join the main forest drive along the valley floor. We then keep to this track all the way back to Allerston. From (13) we are on the main LPC section of the walk and at (14) the short circuit route joins in. Once we reach Allerston, we can refresh ourselves before visiting Ebberston Church and Hall.

CAUTION
Free
range children
and animals
Please drive slowly.
[c]

Exploring
Lake Pickering

from
previous
walk

13

WOODHEAD BROS
WARREN HOUSE FARM
[e]

12
Givendale
Head Farm

11

Givendale Dyke

10

N

path
diversion

Scamridge Dykes
G
9

Scamridge Slack

Malton
Cote
S

Pheasant
Hill Farm

Kirkdale
Bldgs

Concessionary route by kind permission
of landowner, in no way granting any
general right of public access.

14

2000
[a]

Givendale Head Farm
[d]

Kirk
Dale

Allerston Beck

Netherby Dale

G 8

7 G

Chafer
Wood

Springs
P

Kings House 82
[b]

Spring

Ebberston
Hall

Cairn
Pinfold

P
6

A170

Mill
(disused)

P

Allerston

2
G G

3
G

Bloody Beck

4
G

Ebberston

A170

P

P

CAYLEY ARMS
FREE HOUSE
[f]

1

Mill
Pond

S
5

0   1km
0   0.5 mile

Reproduced with
kind permission of
Ordnance Survey
© Crown Copyright
NC/02/4230

Ebberston Hall

Special Interest - WALK 19

Ebberston Hall

Ebberston Hall has been variously described as a Palladian Gem, a villa, a chateau, England's smallest stately home, a shooting box, a folly and, by its architect, a 'Rustick Edifice'. Whatever your choice of phrase, it's a delight not to be missed. The Hall was built in 1718 by William Thompson, MP for Scarborough and the Warden of the Mint. The original design had included a square cupola on top of the roof but this was demolished in 1905.

In 1814 Ebberston was sold to George Osbaldestone, the sporting 'Squire of England'. He could supposedly outride, outshoot and outbox any man of his weight in the country. He had plans for enlarging the house but these never materialised through lack of money. One of his notable sporting feats, done for a bet, was a ride from York to London in under 12 hours, changing horses every 10 miles. Later, when he was heavily in debt, he used to take his furniture to the local inn and sell it, piece by piece, for drink. His last piece of furniture was sold in the 1920s.

The house fell badly into disrepair but has recently seen major restoration so that it is now free from dry rot and has been made structurally safe. A major feature of the Hall is its water garden. This is fed by natural springs which supply a series of pools on three different levels.

The dining room looks out on to the garden and was originally built as an open, colonnaded loggia but cold northerly winds blowing down from the moors soon changed this plan and the area was covered in. At the time of writing Ebberston Hall is not generally open to the public.

Chafer Wood Nature Reserve in Netherby Dale includes **King Alfred's Cairn** which was erected in 1970 to mark the site of a natural limestone cave where, according to local legend, a Saxon king took refuge after battle. The cave was excavated in the 1950s and was to found to contain human remains linked with Neolithic burial rites. Around the cairn area are found flowers such as cowslip, rockrose, salad burnet and pyramidal orchid, typical of limestone grassland. On the eastern slopes of the valley ash-dominated woodland is found with a wide variety of flowers and birds including warblers, redstart, blackcap and woodpeckers. The **Netherby Dales Dykes** are a Scheduled Ancient Monument.

St John's Church, Allerston contains fragments of Norman carving built into its walls suggesting that the church was rebuilt in the Middle Ages. The 15th century battlemented tower has recently been extensively repaired.

St Mary's Church, Ebberston is separated from its village and would seem to have suffered from subsidence, since its floor slopes from west to east. The arcades and south doorway are Norman but major rebuilding in 1876 shaped the church as it is now.

Special Interest - WALK 20

The Dykes

The word 'dyke' may be misleading because it can refer to a hedge, wall, bank or a combined ditch-and-bank feature. Spratt and Harrison identify three sorts of prehistoric dyke: those which marked out major farming 'estates', those which defined large tribal areas and those called cross-ridge dykes which were probably built later to sub-divide the large farming estates into smaller units.

Yorkshire's prehistoric dykes are important because structures like these are rarely seen in continental Europe. In Britain only Wessex and the Yorkshire Wolds have larger concentrations. The dykes are estimated to date from about 1,000BC and the most spectacular lie east of Newton Dale where they form well-defined ridges across the Tabular Hills. At one time they were thought to be defensive fortifications but today they are generally regarded as having been boundary earthworks. Oxmoor, Scamridge, Cockmoor and Netherby Dale Dykes are all included in the LPC walks. The dykes run in a generally southern direction from the high land above Troutsdale scarp edge. The exceptional size of the inspiring Scamridge system, running in a great arc from Cockmoor to Ebberston, poses a problem and suggests that this may have been not just a local boundary line but a major tribal division. The great Double Dykes near Studford Ring (Walk 8) are also thought to be an example of this kind of political boundary.

The Cockmoor Dykes are in some ways even more fascinating because they are made up of two apparently different types of dyke. Six large dykes and up to fourteen smaller banks have been counted and it is noticeable how the old 'Royal Road' cuts through the larger prehistoric dykes but not through the smaller ones to the west. This suggests that the smaller ones were built after the road. The area was very important for rabbit warrening in the 18th and early 19th centuries and so it is possible that these smaller embankments may have been constructed as rabbit warrens.

Wydale Hall seems to have begun as a manor house in the later Middle Ages although the oldest part of the present building dates from about 1780 and was constructed by the Cayley family. They owned the property until the beginning of the 20th Century. In the First World War, Wydale was used as a hospital and then in the Second World War it was requisitioned by the army as well as seeing service as a P.O.W. camp. After the War, Wydale was leased to the Sisters of the Order of the Holy Paraclete who used the house for a short time as a school and later as a retreat centre. Then in the 1960s Wydale was taken over by the Diocese of York and today hosts conferences and courses in addition to functioning as a retreat centre. The Emmaus Centre, the converted and modernised stable block, caters specially for youth groups on restricted budgets. One of the particular attractions of the Hall grounds is the selection of

fine cedar trees brought from Lebanon, the Himalayas and North Africa in the 19th century.

St Stephen's Church, Snainton had its Norman building demolished in 1835 but the font and old doorway arch were reprieved. A stained glass window comes from Wydale Hall, former home of the Cayleys.

WALK 20
EBBERSTON - WYDALE - SAWDON

Map: Explorer OL 27
S.E.P.:   Chafer Wood (899832) or
         Ebberston (899827) or
         Cockmoor Dykes (914868)
Lake Pickering distance: **4.1 miles**
    (incl extension one-way to Wood Gate)
Large circular walk distance: **10.4 miles**
    (excl extension to Wood Gate)
Shorter walk alternatives:
    via Wy Dale   **8.4 miles** and
    via Cliff Lane   **5.6 miles**
Special interest:
    Scamridge Dykes, Wydale Hall, Chafer Wood

This walk goes across a number of the dry dales which are characteristic of the limestone Tabular Hills. As well as reflecting on the prehistoric earthworks of the region, we visit the dale where Sir George Cayley carried out his aeronautical experiments.

We can park either at the designated parking spaces at Chafer Wood or in the village car park along the back lane in Ebberston. From the latter, we leave the village on the grassy hedged Scarth Lane track following the waymarks past the golf driving range (hunting for mis-hit balls in the adjacent fields is an excellent diversion for youngsters) to the road at (1).

Bearing left, we follow the road to the A170 and turn right into Snainton. At the fire station we note the old pinfold and may wish to try to puzzle out the 'Equation of Time' graph on the millennium sundials. Here the short walk option can turn left up Cliff Lane but the main route goes on past St Stephen's Church with its detached Norman doorway arch. We can turn down Station Road to visit the Methodist Chapel before continuing along the High Street to the war memorial at Lairs Lane.

We go up the lane, leave the built-up area and then turn right at the crosspaths (2). Admiring the views of the 'Lake', we come to the gate at (3) and then go left through the gate but first stay up near the top of the valley side before going gently down into Wy Dale. This pleasant dry valley retains its parkland character and when we go through another gate at (4), we have to bend right up the track and must not miss the waymarked path on our right (5) which takes us through trees towards Wydale Hall. The p.r.o.w. bends left through a gate and we continue round through a further gate to Wydale Lane (6).

Crossing the road, we follow the path just to our left into Brompton Dale, the location for George Cayley's aeronautical experiments. By the gate (7) we go down left to the dew-pond before bearing left again on the p.r.o.w which is waymarked up the valley. Then forking right, we pass a deep stone-capped well and come to the wide bridleway at Cote Head Farm. It's decision time again: those completing all of the LPC need to do a short out-and-back detour to Wood Gate lane in order to make the link between this walk and the next.

From Cote Head we carry on along the broad track to the crossing at (8). The short length walk goes straight on and crosses Wy Dale valley again; the long and medium walks turn right. At first the path is hedged but soon we are following limestone walls. Waymarks next direct us diagonally over one amazingly stony field. We aim for a clump of trees and then bend right alongside the wall to reach the gates at (9). The piles of stones we pass have been hand-lifted off the field by the farmer. A minor diversion sends us through the bigger gate on the right and then on to Moorsome Farm. Passing to the left of the farm, we join Snainton Lane.

Going right on the road, we walk to the head of the lane and investigate (and count?) the exceptionally well-preserved Scamridge Dykes. We can also continue down the road a little way to catch a glimpse of Troutsdale.

From the car park at the Dykes, we take the Link Path going WNW next to, and then into, the Cockmoor Hall Plantation. The route may turn muddy as we carry on to the bridleway turning at (10). This is the point we came to from a southerly direction on Walk 19 and we now retrace that route but in the opposite direction. Walking south, we skirt round the tree-covered dykes (11), join the road at Malton Cote and come to the entrance to Chafer Wood Nature Reserve (12).

We enter the reserve and go to the gate used on Walk 19 but this time, instead of going up the valley side and taking the path at the top of the trees, we carry on straight ahead along the path on the bottom of the valley. This really is a gem of a sunken woodland path; fallen trees add to the excitement but I'll leave you to discover its delights for yourself. Leaving the wood by the roadside car parks, we go straight on into Ebberston.

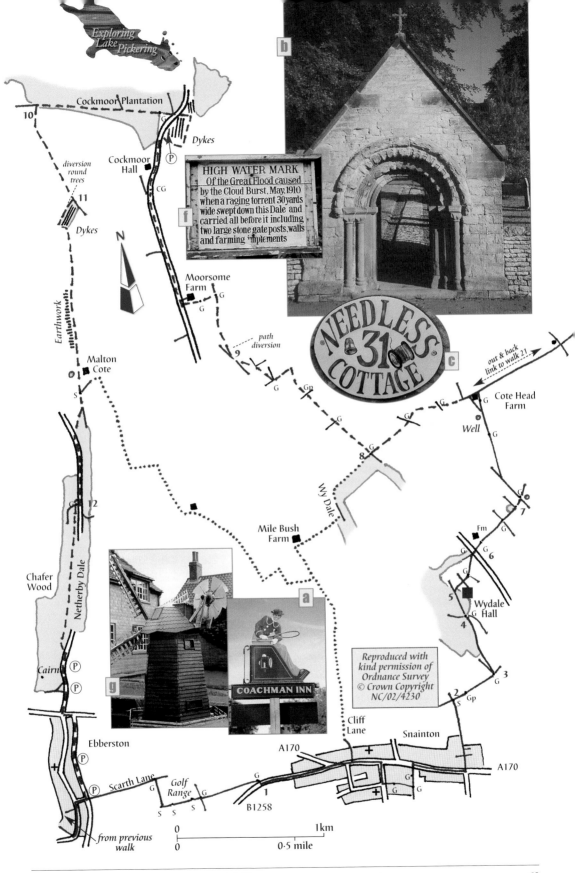

WALK 21
SAWDON - BROMPTON
- HUTTON BUSCEL

Map: Explorer OL 27
S.E.P.: Brompton (945818) or Hutton Buscel
         (973841) or Sawdon (943849)
Lake Pickering distance: **5.6 miles**
Circular walk distance
    (incl Sawdon loop):   **12.0 miles**
    (excl Sawdon loop):   **9.0 miles**
Shorter walk alternatives: **6.2 miles;**
    Sawdon loop   **3.4 miles**
Special interest: Sir George Cayley

This walk links four settlements along the edge of the Vale of Pickering with Sawdon on the slopes of the Tabulars and there is an optional extra loop into the southern part of Wykeham Forest.

If we start from Sawdon village, we go down Chapel Lane to the crosspaths with Wood Gate (1) – this is the end of the 'missing LPC link' which keenies conscientiously completed on the last walk. Here we go left and follow the broad track with its fine views of 'Lake Pickering' all the way down to the A170.

We turn right and walk into Brompton-by-Sawdon. Just past Cayley Lane (2), on the left side of the road, is the building where George Cayley conducted his aeronautical experiments. Here we turn left down the grass path, then right on the road to bring us to Brompton Church.

From the church, we take the footpath immediately opposite and walk beside the extremely attractive duck ponds. At the houses, our route swings left along the road and then goes straight over the next road and an open grassy area sometimes used as a car park. At the far side we take the track (Acres Lane) to the right of the farm. This leads us to a gate and then a field-side path which passes through a series of hedge gaps to Hudgin Lane (3). Just to our right is the driveway leading to Wykeham Abbey but this is not open to the public, so we turn left instead and walk on the quiet lane to the A170 at (4). The hummocky land on our right is part of the terminal moraine which marked the limit of North Sea ice as it pushed westwards into the Vale.

Crossing the main road, we turn right and then go left into Ruston. At the village centre road junction we take the middle of the three roads and go to the waymarked Millennium Path on our right (5). This crosses a field and then follows an old railway line to Wykeham. At the finger-post (6), we turn right to visit the Millennium Stone, the restored Ice House and Wykeham Church.

Retracing our steps to (6), we bear right on the path upslope and then have permission from the caravan site owners to walk along the edge of the caravan park to the driveway corner at (7). We continue across the 'Dog release area' ahead of us, taking the second from left of the mown pathways to a gap in the opposite fence. Then we cross ploughland to the stile at the road corner (8). Following the road into Hutton Buscel, we go past the Methodist Chapel to St Matthew's Parish Church and then on to Middle Lane (9).

Turning up the lane, we branch off left at (10). The next mile or so includes several staggered junctions (see map) but we follow the signed p.r.o.w. down to the footbridge over Beedale Beck and then continue along field boundaries and two more tarred lanes to the gap at (11). Here we turn off right and follow Sawdon Beck round field edges to the waymark at (12). We are sent over the stream and then at the next fence need to bear left up the gulley to a gate. Going through and turning right, we come into Sawdon.

The longer walk now turns off right down Low Lane on the first of several routes down to Sawdon Beck. The path drops steeply and we go left at the first junction. Then at the fingerpost we go right, following the beck downstream. At the next fingerpost we turn left up the steep valley side through the trees. Emerging at the top of the wood (13), we cross pasture land to the corner of Cockmoor Plantation. The path continues along the side of the wood and joins Wykeham Lane (14).

We now go left on the road, past some of the Forestry Commission tree nurseries and Research Office and on through the wood to the grassy track at (15). This takes us through the F.C. property, along a field edge and on to another delightful woodland trail. This takes us down to Sawdon beck (16) and, though the pattern of paths may seem complicated, if we follow the signs, we should not get into trouble. We go left on the footpath (not right on the bridleway) criss-cross over the beck, go past an old weir and come to another fingerpost at (17). Here we take the centre of the three paths and carry on straight ahead for about 200m. We should spot the rough steps cut out on our right leading us back up to Sawdon village, but if we miss them we can take the path a little further on which we used at the start of the walk.

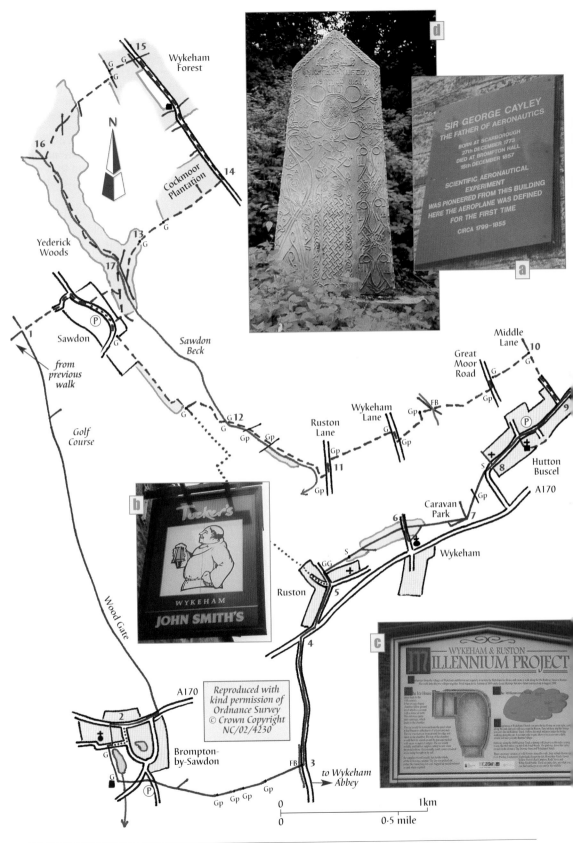

Wykeham Forest

15

16

Cockmoor Plantation

14

Yederick Woods

13

17

N

d

a

SIR GEORGE CAYLEY
THE FATHER OF AERONAUTICS

BORN AT SCARBOROUGH
27TH DECEMBER 1773
DIED AT BROMPTON HALL
15TH DECEMBER 1857

SCIENTIFIC AERONAUTICAL
EXPERIMENT
WAS PIONEERED FROM THIS BUILDING
HERE THE AEROPLANE WAS DEFINED
FOR THE FIRST TIME

CIRCA 1799~1855

Middle Lane
10
Great Moor Road

Sawdon

from previous walk

Sawdon Beck

G 12

Ruston Lane

Wykeham Lane

FB

9

P

Hutton Buscel

8

A170

Golf Course

11

Gp

Caravan Park

7

6

Wykeham

b

Ticker's

WYKEHAM

JOHN SMITH'S

Ruston

5

Wood Gate

4

A170

2

Brompton-by-Sawdon

Reproduced with kind permission of Ordnance Survey © Crown Copyright NC/02/4230

FB 3
to Wykeham Abbey

c

WYKEHAM & RUSTON
MILLENNIUM PROJECT

The Millennium...

0   1km
0   0.5 mile

Special Interest - WALK 21

Sir George Cayley (1773-1857)

George Cayley has been called 'The Father of Aeronautics' and is responsible for the modern theory of aerodynamics. In Brompton village we see the building in which he planned the world's first aeroplanes. The story of his experiments makes fascinating reading. His revolutionary concept was to use a fixed wing model, rather than a flapping wing model, to obtain flight and his first successful glider experiment took place in 1804. This has been described as the first aeroplane although it did not carry humans. Cayley continued his experiments at Brompton Dale with bigger gliders allowing them to fly down from higher to lower land.

By 1849 Cayley's machines had progressed so much that he could report that 'a boy of ten was floated off the ground for several yards on a descending hill'. Then in 1853 at Brompton Dale his coachman was persuaded to become the first person to take part in what is now recognised as the real birth of manned flight. But after his historic glide, the coachman immediately gave his notice claiming that he had been employed to drive, not to fly!

George Cayley died in 1857 and it was nearly half a century later before the Wright Brothers were able to make powered flight a reality.

In addition to his work on aerodynamics Sir George developed caterpillar traction, the bicycle wheel, artificial limbs and armaments. He was also responsible for the idea of the Scalby Sea Cut. This is the overflow channel which takes surplus water from the Derwent out to the North Sea at Scalby and so reduces flooding in Malton. We see this flood control work on Walk 22.

At the time of writing, plans are being made to celebrate the 150th Anniversary of Sir George's flight with a commemorative festival in 2003. Yorkshire's answer to Leonardo da Vinci? Well, perhaps not quite. But certainly George Cayley was an innovative genius.

All Saints Church, Brompton was the location for William Wordsworth's marriage in 1802 and a copy of his marriage entry is on view. The church spire, with 'broaches' at its base, is reminiscent of those found in the Midland counties. A stained glass window in the chancel reproduces Raphael's 'Sermon of St Paul at Athens' from the cartoons in the Sistine Chapel. There is also a beautiful modern window showing a large number of different birds. The south door is interesting; it was thrown into the adjacent pond by Cromwell's men and then later retrieved in 1793 after about 150 years under water.

All Saints Church, Wykeham is a Victorian creation of 1853 which kept the old 14th century tower but gave it a spire and made it the separated gatehouse for the new church.

Wykeham Abbey was a Cistercian nunnery founded about 1153. The present building, dating largely from about 1904, is a stately home.

St Matthew's Church, Hutton Buscel has a Norman tower and the arcades date from the 13th and 15th centuries.

Replica of George Cayley's 'Man Carrier', 1852.

Special Interest - WALK 22

Forge Valley National Nature Reserve

As Lake Hackness overflowed at the end of the Ice Ages, it ran south cutting the spectacular Forge Valley gorge. West and East Ayton stand on the delta laid down by the meltwater as it emerged into the Vale of Pickering. The flood water is then thought to have passed westwards along the edge of the Pickering ice laying down a terrace of sands and gravels. These can be seen in the quarry at 985850.

The woodlands (not the individual trees) are thought to be 6,000 years old and form a link with the ancient wildwood which once covered most of England. The valley is named after the 14th century iron forges which used charcoal made in the woods. Primroses and dog's mercury are resplendent in spring. If there is time, do visit the bird-watchers' car park and you will be certain to see blue and great tits as well as perhaps coal tits, nuthatches and tree creepers. But you have to be a real expert to distinguish a marsh tit from a willow tit - I gave up! Redpolls and siskins flock together in autumn to feed on alder cones and otters are re-establishing themselves in the river.

St Peter's Church, Hackness was founded originally in 680 as a nunnery set up by St Hilda, Abbess of Whitby. Its greatest treasure is its 9th century Anglian cross, discovered in the 1830s being used as a gate-post. It is carved with scroll-work and bears inscriptions probably in honour of a former abbess. The inscriptions are in Latin, runes and Celtic Ogham script but only those in Latin can be interpreted. Nevertheless, the variety of scripts suggests a considerable mix of the Roman and Celtic traditions of the early church. Other fragments of Anglo-Saxon carved stones have recently been found in village gardens. The nunnery was destroyed by the Danes in the 9th century but the church was rebuilt again before the arrival of the Normans. Part of the chancel arch dates from c.900. The south arcade is Norman. Other treasures include the splendid font cover (c.1480), the chancel misericords and a Jacobean pulpit.

The present **Hackness Hall** dates from 1795 when the owner decided to pull down the old manor house and build anew. The entire village, apart from church and school, was moved a mile or so down the road in order to make way for extended gardens and an orangery – they did that sort of thing in those days. Later the old monastic fish ponds were enlarged to make the present lake and the mill was constructed.

Ayton Castle is better described as a medieval 'fortified house'. A true 'castle' had the needs of defence as its main priority and residential comfort as a secondary consideration. Fortified houses, on the other hand, had domestic convenience as their prime concern and protection against, for example, Scottish raiding parties, as a subsidiary importance. Some Yorkshire fortified houses had moats for protection. Others like Ayton Castle were built as tower houses. Constructed near the end of the14th century, Ayton 'Castle' had a typical pele-tower design and was a rectangular house with three storeys: basement cellar and kitchen, hall on the first floor and private apartments above. Today we can see little more than the remains of two of the walls.

WALK 22
HUTTON BUSCEL –
WEST AYTON –
FORGE VALLEY

Map: Explorer OL 27
S.E.P.: Hutton Buscel (973841) or
West Ayton (988847) or
Hazel Head (984876)
Lake Pickering distance: **8.1 miles**
Circular walk distance: **11.1 miles**
Shorter walk alternatives:
(turning at Old Man's Mouth)
5.2 miles or
(turning at Cockrah) **8.6 miles**
Special interest:
Forge Valley NNR, Hackness Church,
Sea Cut, Ayton Castle

On this walk we follow one side of the
nationally important Forge Valley Woods, do a
mini-circuit around Hackness and then follow
the River Derwent on a different path down
Forge Valley.

From Hutton Buscel, we walk NE through the
village and down the hill towards Mount
Pleasant, but turn left up Far Lane (1) and then
branch off right on the bridleway at (2). This
track leads us along and down to the road at (3).
Here we go right and walk round the road
corner up to the p.r.o.w. on our left. This takes
us round two sides of a field to Cockrah Road;

we turn right for 45m before going left on the
track past the screened caravan site. This hedged
path turns sharp left at the field corner (4) and
then runs by the side of the field to the trees at
(5).

Two paths are visible as we enter the trees. We
take the one on the left and stay up along the
top edge of the valley just inside the Forge Valley
Woods. The path is easy to follow but at (6) it
divides. The more obvious path drops down to
the River Derwent and this is the short circuit
route. The longer walks bear up left and
continue, still inside the wood, to Spikers Hill.

We then briefly leave the trees before re-entering and descending steeply.

After emerging once more (7), the p.r.o.w. goes gently down over pasture land, past North Stile Cottage and then a track leads to the path junction just before the buildings at Cockrah Foot (8).

Here we have another choice of route. The medium length walk turns almost back on itself and takes the path down valley alongside the River Derwent. It allows us to view the Weir Head sluice where George Cayley's Sea Cut takes off surplus River Derwent floodwater.

The long walk (and the full LPC) carries on along the road and at Wrench Green (9) we turn right to follow the track and hedge to the bridge over the Derwent. Then we join the road at (10) and a left turn takes us into Hackness, past the mill pond and round to St Peter's Church. A visit here is a must before we continue on the road past Hackness Hall to Greengate Wood.

The path leaves the road at (11) and swings round right before entering the trees over a stile and taking us up to pleasant 'hidden' wooded track. We come out at a farm track (12) and, bearing right, continue past Suffield Ings and on to yet another wood, Hawthorn Wood. This is as

delightful as the others we have been through and when we come out, we veer left over grassland down to a gate and, turning right, take the track which forks left down to Mowthorpe Farm. Diverted round the farm, we come out on Mowthorp Road.

Turning left and crossing the bridge over the impressive Sea Cut, we continue to the Hazel Head car park just before the road T-junction (13). (Here the day circular walk leaves the main LPC.) It is possible to follow an indistinct path alongside the river from here but we may prefer to use the road to the highly recommended bird-watchers' car park before carrying on to cross the river over the footbridge at Old Man's Mouth picnic site (14). The path running immediately next to the Derwent is one of North Yorkshire's most delightful riverside walks and is now duckboarded along its previously boggy course.

When the river swings away left (15) we stay by the fence. Then after leaving the Nature Reserve the path goes over grazing land and we pass the remains of Ayton Castle before coming into West Ayton village and returning to our cars. If we have left them in Hutton Buscel, the pavement beside the A170 gives safety from fast traffic.

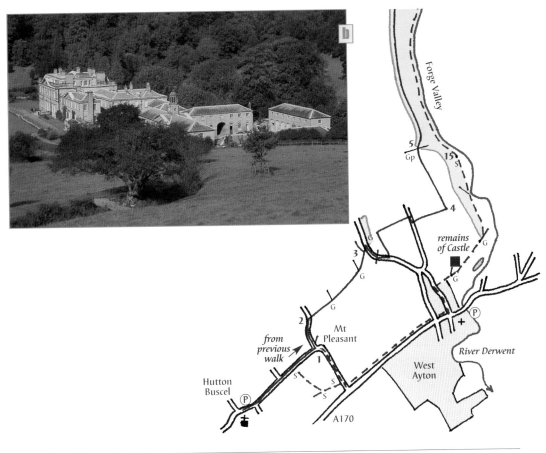

WALK 23
FORGE VALLEY – FALSGRAVE MOOR

Map: Explorer OL 27
S.E.P.:   Hazel Head car park (984876) or
         Thoxenby Mere (010887)
Lake Pickering distance: **6.1 miles**
Circular walk distance: **10.1 miles**
Shorter walk alternative: **6.6 miles**
Special interest:
    Seamer Beacon, Harland Mount, Raincliffe
    Woods

As well as passing through some fine woodlands, this walk goes over open land on which there is much evidence of prehistoric occupation.

To complete the LPC route, we start from Hazel Head car park, turn right on the road and then follow the direction to 'Raincliffe Woods and Lady Edith's Drive'. This brings us to Green Gate car park. Here we turn back on ourselves and take the track signed 'public footpath' (not the bridleway) into the Forge Valley Nature Reserve. Avoiding an early branch left up a stepped path, we keep straight on and then at the path fork (1) bear left and rise steeply to the top edge of the valley side. The path then keeps to the wall and eventually leads down from Ruston Cliff to the road at (2).

From here we must walk on the roadside for a little way but at the weir on the River Derwent we can use a riverside path for a few hundred metres before we have to climb steps back up to the road.

To visit East Ayton's lovely honey-coloured church we stay on the road to the A170 and then turn left through the village. After visiting the church we turn left on to Racecourse Road and immediately left again into Moor Lane. We follow this road to the track branching left at (3). About 200m later (4) we swing left round the top of a wooded ravine and then bend right along the hedged path.

When we come to the track at (5) we turn right past Whin Covert and go as far as the 5-way junction at (6). We bear NE on the track between two big barns, cross Irton Moor, skirt past the ancient tumulus on Hagworm Hill and go as far as the second telecommunications mast at (7). Here the short walk goes down the steep slope ahead on the p.r.o.w. to Raincliffe.

The long walk turns right along Row Brow to the stile at (8) and here a permissive path takes us to the superbly sited Seamer Beacon on our right. When we leave the Beacon, we can either retrace our steps or follow the gorse hedge to bring us back to the main track at (9).

Continuing towards the M.O.D. Wireless Station, we branch off left (10) about 300m before the main road on the path to Jacob's Mount. When we come to the A170, we cross to the stile opposite and then continue round the right-hand side of the caravan site. Then we descend the steps and follow the path through the trees and over a field to the path junction at (11). Here we turn back left on the bridleway up to Harland Mount from where we get fine views across to Scarborough.

Crossing the A170 again (12) we follow the sign just to our right to Woodlands Road. The path stays by the side of the recently restored hedge and leads us past the entrance to Woodlands Cemetery. A waymarked diversion takes us round Row Farm but then after crossing a small beck we should be prepared in winter for two boggy fields before we reach the lane at (13). Now we turn right and walk down towards Throxenby Mere.

Going left on the road to the far end of the Mere (14), we take the path on our left and cross to the other side of the water. At the foot of the slope there are several paths; we take the one veering slightly right and going up the hill into Raincliffe Woods. After avoiding a side path on the left, our route later swings right and then, immediately after a disused quarry, does a sharp left turn. We go up steeply for 50m to a bench on the main track through the woods (15). Here we go right and for a couple of miles there is a wonderful woodland trail taking us back to Green Gate. Raincliffe Meadow is an open area being partially replanted but providing we keep to the main track, there should be no navigation difficulties.

Special Interest – WALK 23

St John the Baptist Church, East Ayton has a Norman font and Norman beakhead carvings on the church doorway but there have been many alterations through the centuries, including the installation of the unusual Venetian-style east window.

Ice from the North Sea rode up on to Seamer Moor leaving morainic material at Hagworm Hill and Baron Albert's Tower. A lobe of ice moving up the line of the Sea Cut dumped moraine at Thorn Farm (985882).

Seamer Beacon with its surrounding tumuli, ditches and banks is an important Bronze Age site. Baron Albert's Tower was built overlooking the former racecourse.

Harland Mount Nature Reserve includes a wildflower meadow and semi-natural woodland.

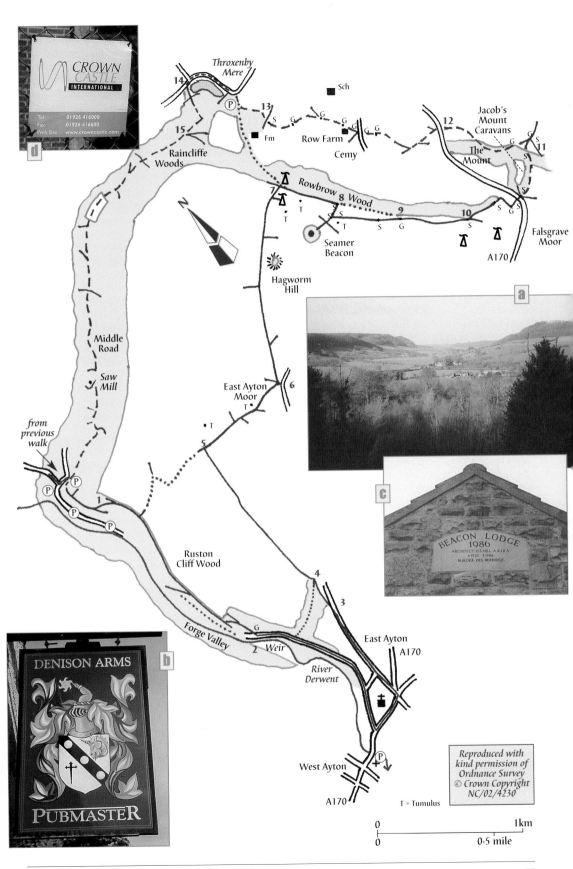

Throxenby Mere

Sch

Jacob's Mount Caravans

14

P

13

S   G   G   G   G

12

15

Raincliffe Woods

Fm

Row Farm

Cemy

11

The Mount

S

Falsgrave Moor

7

Rowbrow 8 Wood

9

10

S   G

A170

T

S   S   T

S   G

S

Seamer Beacon

Hagworm Hill

N

Middle Road

Saw Mill

East Ayton Moor

T

6

from previous walk

T

5

P   P

P

1

P

a

Ruston Cliff Wood

c

BEACON LODGE
1986
ARCHITECT D.S. HILL A.R.I.B.A

4

3

Forge Valley

G

East Ayton

A170

2   Weir

River Derwent

West Ayton

P

A170

T = Tumulus

0   1km

0   0·5 mile

WALK 24
FALSGRAVE MOOR – OSGODBY (and SCARBOROUGH)

Map: Explorer 301
S.E.P.:   Edge Dell (030855) or
         The Mere (034856) or
         Oliver's Mount (039869)
Lake Pickering distance: **5.2 miles**
Circular walk distance: **11.4 miles**
Shorter walk alternatives: **5.3 miles;**
                              7.1 miles

Special interest:
   Scarborough, Oliver's Mount, The Mere

This walk, which includes several short hilly sections, leads us round the southern outskirts of Scarborough to the North Sea coast and the Cleveland Way. Parking is not practicable at the place where the LPC joins in from the last walk, so it is better to start the day circular walk from one of the sites shown on the map.

If we start from Edge Dell (1) where there is plenty of space available along the side road, we come out to the A64, turn right and follow the footpath to the large roundabout at (2). Going left here, we take the drive signposted to High Deepdale but then at (3) we fork left on the farm track. We have to cross a ploughed area to the field corner at (4). Here the short walk goes left towards Oliver's Mount. The long itinerary turns right to go along the top edge of Deep Dale (it's well-named). If visibility is good, we get fine panoramic views over to the Wolds ahead of us.

At (5) we turn left on the bridleway going by the side of the houses to Manor Farm. Here we go right-left on to Osgodby Lane and continue to the Poachers Barn pub where we leave the road and follow the path to the A165 at (6). Crossing over, the path takes us to the cliffed coast and we turn left on to the Cleveland Way.

The next two miles follow the Cleveland Way. Parts of the cliffs are thickly vegetated; in other parts slumping has exposed the rock beneath the boulder clay.

When we come to the car park (7) we see the results of the cliff stabilisation work which was carried out after the 1993 landslip which destroyed the Holbeck Hall Hotel. (Here, if necessary, it is possible to take a short-cut along Sea Cliff Road and up to Oliver's Mount)

To complete the full route, we drop down and then carry on along the tarred path, past the outdoor pool to the first Cliff Lift … but intrepid walkers will be relieved to know that there is a stepped pedestrian ascent up the cliff face immediately next to the mechanised tramway!

On the Esplanade we go right and then turn down St Martin's Avenue (look up left) to visit the Church with its excellent information display. Then we carry on to the main Filey Road (A165), go left as far as Queen Margaret's Road, turn right to the tarred path leading off left and take this up to Weaponness Drive. Here we take the stepped path opposite up through the trees to Oliver's Mount with its War Memorial and picnic site. On a good day, the view is great.

The walk continues on the road round the west side of the Mount, dropping steeply through trees to the road bend at (8). Steps now lead down left past a car park and then we bear right to The Mere. Paths run on both sides of this lake; we can choose whichever we prefer. Then at the end of The Mere, we come out on to the road and, turning left to cross Seamer Road, we bear slightly right into Edgehill Road. This takes us past Scarborough F.C. ground to the signposted, tarred path going left at (9).

From here we pass through Falsgrave Leisure Village and then turning right at the end of the caravans (10) we follow the grassy track to the path crossing at (11).

Now we take the path, walked the opposite way on Walk 23, going back left to Jacob's Mount caravan park and on to the A170 road. Then turning left for 250m, we reach the track (12) leading to Seamer Moor House Farm. We follow this track and then the marked diversion round the farm brings us to (13). We have to cross the corner of the field to reach the stile in the fence overlooking the gorse-covered valley of Edge Dell.

The next section may be a little adventurous. Bearing right over the stile, the p.r.o.w. slopes off left almost immediately down the steep side of the valley. But the path is narrow and may have gorse bushes crowding in. However, it will bring us down to the houses and our starting point at the end of the valley. (Possible route realignments are being negotiated for this section.)

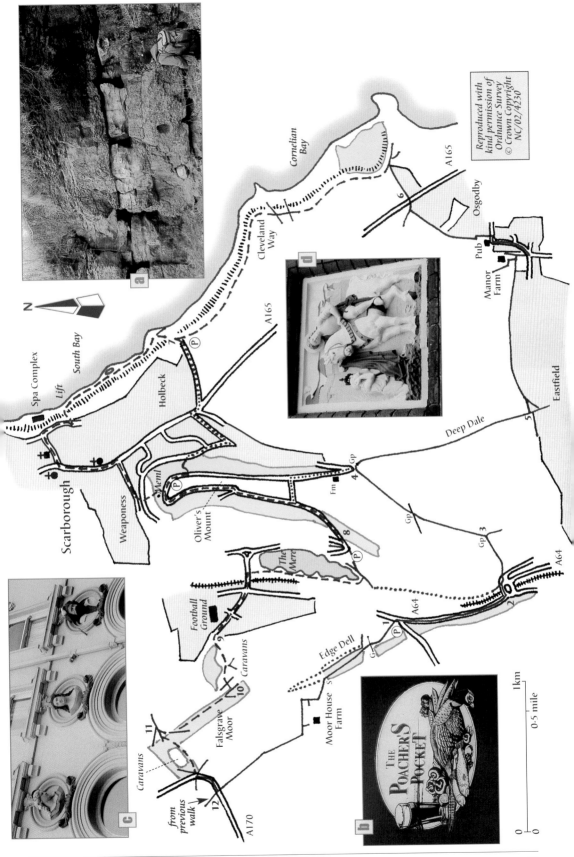

a

d

N

Cornelian Bay

Cleveland Way

A165

6

A165

Osgodby

Pub

Manor Farm

Eastfield

South Bay

Spa Complex

Lift

Holbeck

Deep Dale

5

Scarborough

Weaponess

Mem

Oliver's Mount

Fm

Gp

4

Gp

Gp

3

A64

8

The Mere

A64

2

Football Ground

9

Edge Dell

Gp

P

1

Caravans

10

Falsgrave Moor

Moor House Farm

b

11

Caravans

from previous walk

12

A170

c

Reproduced with kind permission of Ordnance Survey © Crown Copyright NC/02/4250

0 — 0.5 mile — 1km

THE POACHER'S POCKET

Scarborough

Snippets from the Tourist Office brochure:
Did you know that

- the name of Oliver's Mount may be derived from the mistaken belief that Oliver Cromwell placed batteries here during the siege of Scarborough Castle
- Wood End Museum displays the Giant Tunny – the British record tuna fish caught off Whitby in 1949
- the Rotunda Museum contains finds from the internationally important Mesolithic lakeside settlement of Star Carr, an exhibit of Gristhorpe Man (a Bronze Age tree trunk burial) as well as Scarborough's original pancake bell
- when Members of Parliament wish to resign, they apply for the Chiltern Hundreds and are appointed alternately to the Chiltern Hundreds or to Northstead Manor. The ancient manor of Northstead lies beneath the lake in Peasholm Park
- Marine Drive, linking North and South Bays, took 10 years, 10 months and 10 days to build and was finished in 1908?

St Martin's Church on the town's Heritage Trail has a pre-Raphaelite interior and windows and a 'gem of a pulpit'. The church display records that in the 19th century St Martin's was a rare example of an Anglo-Catholic Church in Evangelical Yorkshire.

WALK 25
OSGODBY - GRISTHORPE
(straight along coast)

Map: Explorer 301
S.E.P.: Osgodby (058852) or
        Cayton Bay (069841) or
        Gristhorpe (088820)
Lake Pickering distance: **3.4 miles**
Circular walk distance: **6.7 miles**
Special interest:
   Cayton Bay, North Sea coastal cliffs

This short stretch along the Cleveland Way could be done as an out-and-back walk using public transport to return to the start of the walk but it is possible to do an egg-timer figure-of-eight route as described below. The best parking is in the middle of the walk by Cayton Bay Holiday village, though it is also possible to park either in Osgodby or Gristhorpe. Cayton Sands are best walked at low tide. The route description assumes we are beginning at Osgodby where the last section of the LPC finished.

From the A165 we follow the track we used on the last walk to lead us to the Cleveland Way and then turning right we take the National Trail through the wooded N.T. Cayton Cliff and Tenants' Cliff property. We follow the acorns and ignore sidetracks. The path then becomes more open as we continue round to Lebberston Cliff. We need to be careful in case of possible landslip disturbance but the route stays along the cliff top and we soon reach the finger post (1) directing us right through the Blue Dolphin caravan park towards Gristhorpe.

We follow Stonepit Lane as it bends right (2) and runs parallel to the A165. Then we turn right again (3) on the tarred drive to Mount Pleasant Farm and carry on to the cliff path (4) where we walked earlier in the day. Here we go left and retrace steps as far as the path to the car park (5) but at this point turn down right to Cayton Sands. There is now a fine beach walk to the far end of the bay.

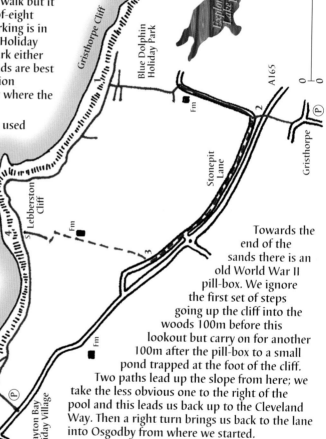

Towards the end of the sands there is an old World War II pill-box. We ignore the first set of steps going up the cliff into the woods 100m before this lookout but carry on for another 100m after the pill-box to a small pond trapped at the foot of the cliff. Two paths lead up the slope from here; we take the less obvious one to the right of the pool and this leads us back up to the Cleveland Way. Then a right turn brings us back to the lane into Osgodby from where we started.

Special Interest

Although off the route of the walk, **Cayton Church** with its Norman doorway, arches and font can be visited at the end of the day if we travel along the B1261. Killerby **Stained Glass Centre** also lies along this road.

Special Interest - WALK 26

Somehow **Filey** manages to maintain its old fishing village charm while at the same time being a holiday beach lover's delight. Walk 26 allows us to visit a number of places of interest highlighted in the town's Heritage Trail.

Filey Dams is the last remaining freshwater marsh of any significant size in the region and is an important staging post for migrant birds, especially waders. Lesser yellowlegs, Baird's sandpiper and black-winged stilt have all been recorded. So too have hoopoe and in all, over 200 species have been observed since 1985. The freshwater reserve affords habitat for a wide range of flowering plants as well as dragon flies and 20 varieties of butterfly.

Filey Museum was originally two thatched cottages and is the oldest domestic building (1696) in the town. Many of the fishermen who used to live in this part of Filey were self-sufficient, growing their own vegetables and keeping a few animals as well as catching fish. Coble Landing is the quayside where Filey's 'cobles' (open fishing boats) are hauled ashore by tractor.

St Oswald's Church stands above the beach where the fishing boats land. Dedicated to St Oswald it is tempting to think that the saint landed here and preached the gospel in the 7th century. The church is long and low with a squat central tower, but the outside hardly prepares us for the surprising interior. The building is in two halves which do not fit together. A Norman doorway leads to a very narrow nave, built around 1180, with supports for a western tower which was never completed. East of the nave, and separated from it, is the splendid tower crossing and a spacious chancel and transepts built in the early English style about 1230. It was evidently planned to finish the new church by replacing the old nave but this was never done. Two sedilia, an ancient stone altar table and a miniature carving of a boy bishop (c.1250) are among the church's other valuable possessions. Outside, various comic heads, an old sundial and a fishy weathervane are worth investigation.

Below the church, in the **Ravine,** is the site of one of the springs in the area which were a source of fresh water used by Dutch fishermen who rolled their barrels up from the beach to collect water supplies when they were fishing off the Yorkshire coast.

Carr Naze is the site of a Roman signal station, one of several built along the coast to give warnings of raids from across the North Sea. Excavations in 1993-94 showed that the station had been garrisoned until the very last years of Roman Britain in the early 5th century. In 1996 severe storms caused the removal of sand from the **Brigg** and the exposure of dozens of Roman coins from AD 138. These were found close to the stone-based jetty which juts out from the Brigg but is only exposed at very low tides. The find gave support to the theory that the jetty was part of a Roman harbour at Filey.

Snippets from the Town Guide:
Did you know that

- in 1274 the Burgesses of Scarborough stole a great whale from Filey
- in 1934 the Daily Telegraph reported the alleged sighting of a two-humped, saucer-eyed, 30 feet long, 8-feet high Loch Ness type monster in Filey Bay
- in 1990 probably the last of the Filey Flither girls (who used to go out to collect limpets for long-line fishing bait) died aged 104?

St Thomas' Church, Gristhorpe was constructed in 1897 from corrugated iron transported in sections by train from London. Built in memory of Brian Beswick who died from diphtheria, the church cost £102.

FILEY'S ROCKET POLE

This pole is one of several on the Yorkshire coast which was used to simulate rescues from stricken cargo ships.

The Filey Volunteer Life Saving Rocket Company, formed in 1872, practised rescue techniques by firing a line towards one of their members, positioned at the top of the pole.

This practice continued until the 1960's when improvements in navigational equipment rendered the Company redundant.

THE POLE WAS RESTORED BY FILEY BRIGG ORNITHOLOGICAL GROUP IN 2001 WITH FUNDS FROM FILEY COMMUNITY CHEST.

WALK 26
GRISTHORPE –
MUSTON (and FILEY)

Map: Explorer 301
S.E.P.: Gristhorpe (088820) or
         Filey (120812) or Muston (100797)
Lake Pickering distance: **2.6 miles**
Circular walk distance: **12.0 miles**
   (incl Filey Brigg)
Shorter walk alternatives: **10.4 miles**
   (excl Filey Brigg) and   **3.6 miles**
Special interest:
   Filey Heritage Trail, Filey Dams, Filey Brigg,
   St Oswald's Church

The LPC section of the walk links Gristhorpe Cliff with the Wolds Way (WW) to the west of Muston and the circular walk allows various possible explorations in Filey. The town's Heritage Trail information boards give a wealth of detail about Filey's history.

Parking in Gristhorpe by the village hall, we walk southwards into the village and turn right at the pub (1). We pass St Thomas' Church on our right and soon reach Station Lane. Here we go left. This takes us over the level crossing and then Carr Lane leads us past Magdalen Grange Farm on to a rough track to the bridleway junction at (2).

Turning right for about 300m on a grassy track, we then go left across the bridge over Main Drain and carry on along the farm track to Manor Farm. Crossing straight over Flotmanby Lane the path start to rise gradually as we begin to climb the Wolds. There is a bend right and we carry on by the field edge as far as the gap in the hedge at (3). Here we join the Wolds Way and, turning back left on ourselves and following the fingerpost direction, we cross cropland to the stile in the far corner of the field.

Veering slightly to our left, we now follow a series of stiles leading us gradually downhill to Flotmanby Lane again (4) where we turn right and walk along the road A1039 into Muston. (We shall walk this stretch in reverse on the next walk.) At the end of the village (5) we follow the WW

branching off left from the main road on to a side crescent and up waymarked steps to a stile. We go over two fields to the A165, cross straight over and then continue beside pasture to the edge of Filey (6). The path turns right and joins the main A1039 road.

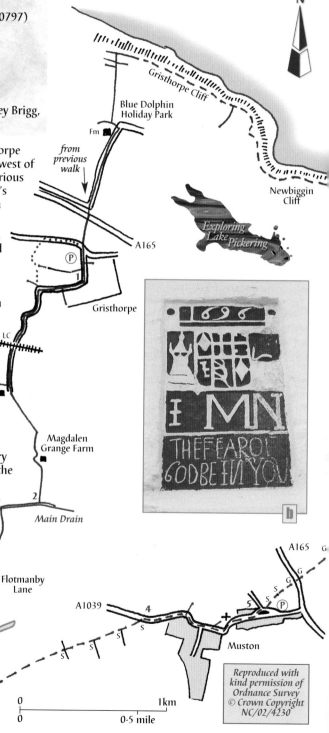

Walking into the town, a recommended detour is to turn first left down Wharfedale and visit Filey Dams Nature Reserve. We can walk round the edge of the marsh and leave the Reserve using the two stiles into Cawthorne Crescent.

Going on into Filey we cross the railway line, bend right and then turn left at the roundabout. At the next mini roundabout we carry on down Church Street but make a slight diversion to visit the museum just off to the right in Queen Street. Then continuing down Church Street we cross the Ravine and come to St Oswald's Church. It is open for visitors and, lying at the extremity of the Oswald-Oswaldkirk axis, should be a focus for all Lake Pickering pilgrims.

At least two options are possible after we leave the church and follow the tarred path at the top of the Ravine to the cliff top at (7). We may choose to stay up and follow the WW along the top edge of the cliffs past the Country Park and on to Filey Brigg. Alternatively, we can go down the steps to the beach and if the tide is out and the sea not too rough, we can reach the Brigg that way.

We come back to the steps at (8) and these bring us up the cliff face to the paths on top of the narrow peninsula*. If we walk on the north side of the ridge we get fine views of the 'doodles' (eroded rock pools) below us and then we continue past the site of the Roman signal station to where the WW and Cleveland Way join together by the site of the old spa (9).

From this point the rest of the walk is clear – we simply keep to the cliff top Cleveland Way route going past North Cliff and on to Gristhorpe Cliff. Views along his section of the national trial are, not surprisingly, spectacular and the different habitats available among soft clay cliffs, hard rock cliffs and tidal rock pools allow a variety of wildlife to flourish. As we follow the cliff path and approach the Blue Dolphin caravan park we should make sure to look westwards because from here we can see (more or less) right down the length of the Vale of Pickering, with the Wolds on our left and the N.Y.Moors on the right, towards the Coxwold-Gilling Gap in the distance. We walk by the caravans to the finger post directing us left on the path back to Gristhorpe and the start of the walk.

*Note: In early 2003 the steps were closed because of landslips so it is sensible to use the cliff top path rather than the beach.

North Cliff

Filey Field

Spa

Country Park

Filey Brigg

9

8

ravine

Filey Dams

SS

LC

G

6

Sch

A1039

Mus

Filey Bay

Coble Landing

Filey

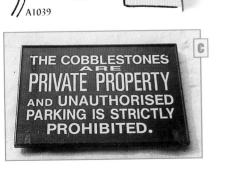

WALK 27
MUSTON - RAVEN DALE

Map: Explorer 301
S.E.P.: Muston (100797)
Lake Pickering distance: **3.2 miles**
Circular walk distance: **10.5 miles**
  (incl Raven Dale and back)
Shorter walk alternatives: **8.0 miles**
  (excl Raven Dale) and   **5.7 miles**

The route for virtually all this circular walk is signed either Wolds Way or Centenary Way and goes over typical Wolds farmland with large fields of wheat, barley, rape-seed or other arable crops.

From the side crescent in Muston we walk through the village along King Street and West Street and go over the stile (1) where the WW leaves the road. Following the field edge, we retrace the route taken on the previous walk back to the bridleway at (2). Turning left, we keep to the edge of another huge field and then cross the road and go past Stockendale Farm. The next bit of the path may be muddy, though the pathside hedge has interesting surprises!

We turn left at (3) and soon the wide grassy path passes down the wooded valley of Stocking Dale. Part of the Dale is a Countryside Stewardship Area and is being returned to grazing. Some scrub has, according to the notice, already been cleared to help open up the Dale. The access agreement allows a full inspection of the site of the Roman Camp (4) though it should be said, there's not a lot immediately apparent on the surface.

At the Camp it's decision time. The day circular walk continues straight ahead but for those keen to complete the full Lake Pickering Circuit it is now necessary to turn off right (into Camp Dale) and do an out-and-back diversion round to the path junction at (5). This will allow the link to be made between the present day walk and the one following (Walk 28). The route is clearly indicated as WW; after a stile and a gate we simply keep to the left-hand side of the fence round to Raven Dale junction (5).

The circular walk continues down Stocking Dale on what is now the Centenary Way. At the stile (6) we go to the right of the hedge, walk round the side of the field and then up the slope before turning off sharp left at (7). A wide grassy path, left clear between crops, leads straight ahead and, whilst the lack of hedgerows inevitably reduces wildlife cover, at least we are given extensive views in all directions. Waymarks guide us round to the right of Field House Farm from where the track becomes tarmacked.

At the road (8) we turn right towards Hunmanby. We go straight over the roundabout and then at the junction (9) we need to turn left along Northgate. However, before we do that we should first go just a short way right to look at Hunmanby Parish Church.

Continuing along Northgate, we reach the end of the houses (10) but carry on in the same direction along the shaly rough track to North Moor Farm. We have to bear right immediately before the farm on a narrow, possibly half-hidden, path to a stile just a few metres further on. From here we go across a cultivated field and then, after another four stiles and a gate, we reach the roundabout on the A165 road.

Turning left, we go as far as the next junction where another left turn takes us back into Muston.

Cherished Memories Of
A LOVING HUSBAND

Special Interest - WALK 27

All Saints Church, Muston was built in 1863 but contains a Norman font.

All Saints Church, Hunmanby has Norman work in the tower and chancel. Pevsner remarks that much of the woodwork from the 1845 restoration 'results in what one might call quite a period interior'.

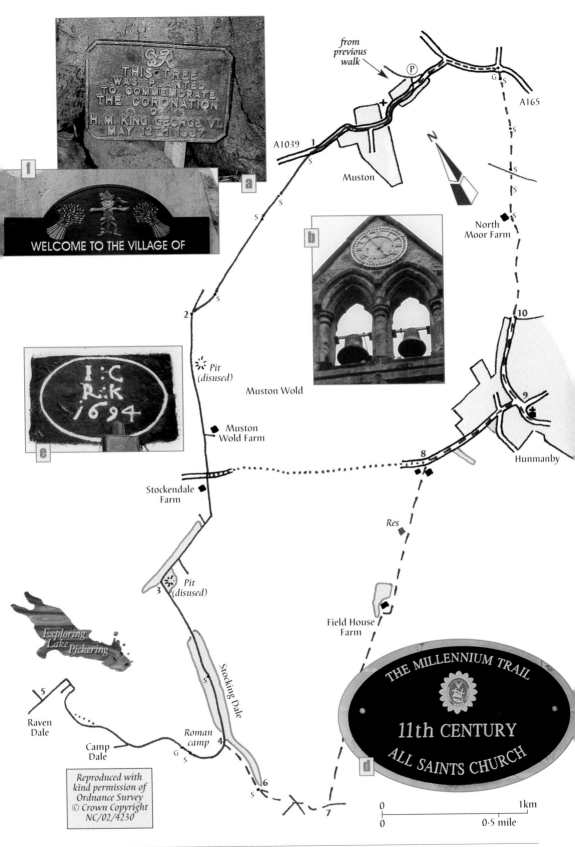

f WELCOME TO THE VILLAGE OF

a GR THIS TREE WAS PLANTED TO COMMEMORATE THE CORONATION OF H.M. KING GEORGE VI MAY 12TH 1937

from previous walk

Ⓟ

G
S
A165

N

A1039 1
S

Muston

✚

b

North Moor Farm
S

S

10

e I:C R:K 1694

Pit (disused)

Muston Wold

Muston Wold Farm

9

✚

8

Hunmanby

Stockendale Farm

Res

Pit (disused)
3

Exploring Lake Pickering

Field House Farm

Stocking Dale
S

d THE MILLENNIUM TRAIL · 11th CENTURY · ALL SAINTS CHURCH

5
Raven Dale

Camp Dale

Roman camp 4
G S

6
S

7

Reproduced with kind permission of Ordnance Survey © Crown Copyright NC/02/4230

0 _____ 1km
0 _____ 0·5 mile

Special Interest - WALKS 27-33

Lake Flixton and Star Carr

As the ice which trapped Lake Pickering gradually melted, deposits of moraine trapped a smaller lake (or series of lakes) known as **Lake Flixton** in the eastern part of the Vale. This has been the subject of much recent research. It has been found that the shoreline of the lake followed approximately the 23 or 24 metre contour and on the edge of the water Early Mesolithic (Middle Stone) Age hunters made their camps at **Seamer** and **Star Carr** about 9,600 years ago. The Star Carr site was excavated in the 1950s and is one of the most important Mesolithic sites in northern Europe. Birch woodland around the lake provided materials for constructing a platform (and possible buildings) and what has been described as the 'earliest known dug-out boat'. In addition the woods were the home of numerous animals and therefore a vital source of food. Red deer was by far the commonest type of meat but wild horse, pig, ox and birds were also eaten. Surprisingly, there was very little fish in the diet. Being relatively shallow, Lake Flixton only lasted a few thousand years and was quickly colonised by reedswamps, saw-sedge beds and the birch, willow and alder trees typical of carr woodland. However, the potential for flooding in the Vale has persisted up to the present day.

John Leland noted (1508) that Seamer still had 'a greate lake on the south west of it'. This gave the town its name ('mere by the sea') and modern O.S. maps show The Mere between the old manor house and the sewage works. Then in 1799 a severe flood was the catalyst for an Act of Parliament allowing Sir George Cayley to construct his Sea Cut to the North Sea and to carry out other drainage and canalisation work in the east of the Vale.

Much later, in the 20th century, despite much improved methods of drainage, flooding in the Vale was still a problem and if the inundations of 1999 and 2000 were anything to do with global climate change, perhaps we should be prepared for similar problems in the future.

However, there is a twist to the story. From a conservationist's point of view, the continued developments in drainage throughout the Vale have been a serious setback to biodiversity. Whilst the drainage procedures have helped to increase food production, the loss of wetland has caused a considerable loss of plant and animal habitat with the consequent loss of species. To a limited extent, artificial wetlands created from the flooded former gravel pits at Wykeham Lakes and Burton Riggs quarry may partially redress the balance but an exciting project was launched in 1997.

The Vale of Pickering Wetlands Project aims to restore and enhance wetland habitats in the region. One centre being developed is at Star Carr, on the edge of the former Lake Flixton. Here the habitats being developed include several of those which existed in the post-glacial period when Lake Flixton was in existence. Previous drainage measures have caused the peat to dry out and shrink, so part of the project involves blocking off existing land drains and controlling the water level with new sluices. Three ponds will be excavated to hold water all year round. The site will be accessible to the public and the long term plan is to create a string of sites from Crossgates to Staxton Brow. These will include Burton Riggs Quarry, Seamer Mere and Flixton Carr Plantation.

Wolds Flowers

The steeper slopes of the chalk scarp and the dry valleys are important for their wild flowers. Sheep and rabbits browsing the grass help keep the taller plants in check and so encourage the smaller, low-lying flowers to flourish. Without this control, invading species like the hawthorn can quickly become established. In summer on areas which are heavily grazed, species such as rock rose, salad burnet, common thyme and hairy violet are all adapted to withstand drought on the shallow soils of the porous chalk. Where the grass is more lightly grazed, several species of orchid can be found.

Wolds Farming

The Agricultural Revolution which took place on the Wolds during the early part of the 19th century owed much to the efforts of Sir Christopher Sykes of Sledmere. Although the steep-sided valleys were too difficult to cultivate, he ploughed up the gently rolling sheep-walks and transformed the landscape by enclosing, fencing, draining and planting. Barley was the favoured new crop. Other landowners followed his example so that within 30 years 'a bleak tract became one of the best cultivated parts of Yorkshire'. Today we see other changes: yellow oil-seed rape, blue borage and bright red wild poppies amidst the corn fields add to the green of young crops and give a patchwork of colour in early summer. Not quite so attractive are the areas of bare earth left by scavenging pigs!

Manufacturing

It seems strange to see a major steel engineering firm in the middle of the countryside but the **Atlas Company** in Sherburn (Walk 29) began as a small enterprise set up by two brothers to make farm buildings like Dutch barns. The company has since greatly expanded. It buys in steel girders and then manufactures them into the pre-fabricated frames for a whole range of buildings. Products are sold in Europe and the company now has offices in the Ukraine.

Although none of the walks goes to the **Knapton Maltings,** the factory is visible for miles around. Initially the Knapton site was chosen in 1952 as a barley drying and storage centre to take grain from the surrounding farmland before sending it on to maltings in West Yorkshire. Closure of these smaller maltings has led to centralisation at the Knapton plant which produces a variety of speciality malts for use in the brewing industry.

Settlement

The study of place names can help us in our understanding of the history of settlement in the Vale of Pickering. Most of the villages are strung out along either the spring line at the base of the Wolds escarpment or the spring line at the foot of the Tabular Hills. Here water, the number one priority for any village, was available. In addition these sites lay above the easily flooded Vale and also gave access to different sorts of farmland above and below the village.

Along the route of the A64/A1039 there is a line of -*ton* settlements at the foot of the Wolds. (There is a similar line of -*ing*, -*ham* and -*ton* sites on the north side of the Vale along the A170.) Though some of these names were later modified by Viking settlers as they took over the villages, the -*ton* endings show they were originally Anglian communities. So places like Ganton, Staxton, Flixton, Folkton and Muston each combine a Viking personal name with the Anglian -*tun*. These hybrid names are sometimes described as the 'Grimston' type. On the other hand, there are many places in Yorkshire where the Scandinavians left the Anglian names unaltered even though their Viking sculptures are clear evidence of their presence. Examples include Hovingham and Lastingham.

However, Scandinavian settlers also left their own place-name marks. Their influence is shown in the -*by* name endings and so on the south side of the Vale we find Willerby, Hunmanby and Flotmanby while along the north side we see Kirkby, Aislaby and Scalby.

It has been suggested that because the -*by* villages occupy less fertile land they were probably settled at a later date after the better land had been taken.

At a later stage still, the Scandinavians set up their -*thorpe* settlements on even less attractive land. (We may have noticed this on the walks in the Howardian Hills.)

Scampston Hall

(Walk 32) has house, garden and park attractions and is open to the public at selected times in the summer (01944 758224 for details). It is the family home of Sir Charles and Lady Legard. The house owes its development to four men in particular, all called William. Sir William St Quintin, 3rd Baronet, was an MP for Hull and built the house around 1700. His nephew William, 4th Baronet, succeeded him and was responsible for moving the road away from the house (hence the awkward bend in the road). It appears he was rather extravagant because he had to flee the country to escape paying his debts. The next William, 5th Baronet, revised the layout of the park in 1773 with advice from Capability Brown. A waterfall and lower lake, which actually looks more like a river, were added and the Palladian Bridge was constructed. The fourth William, William Darby, carried out major alterations to the building in 1801 and we see those results today. However, the Hall has recently undergone extensive repair and has been re-roofed, re-wired and redecorated. Many of the rooms had become dirty with the smoke from coal fires and needed careful cleaning before being restored as near as possible to their original appearance.

Scampston Hall

WALK 28
RAVEN DALE – BINNINGTON BROW

Map: Explorer 301
S.E.P.: Willerby Brow (009779) or
      Willerby Church (008792)
Lake Pickering distance: **4.7 miles**
Circular walk distance: **11.0 miles**
Shorter walk alternatives: **4.5 miles;**
                             8.9 miles

Special interest:
  Lake Flixton and Star Carr

We stay on the pavement through Flixton; Main Street is probably more interesting than Back Lane; and soon come to Folkton. A slight detour to St John's Church is recommended, though it may be locked, and then we come back to the p.r.o.w. at (2). (Note the change from the O.S. map.)

The broad track leads up the chalk face to Hill Top. From here we walk on the right side of the hedge to the telegraph pole at (3). Going left, we walk for another three telegraph poles before

The long LPC section of this walk continues along the WW/CW and there are numerous variations for the circular walks, depending on how far people wish to walk (and how many ups and downs they want to face). On this walk we get fine views across Lake Flixton.

The suggested start for the longest of the circular routes is from Willerby Church and from there we walk eastwards to Folkton, then south up to the WW before turning westwards to go over Flixton and Staxton Wolds. This means we do the bulk of the road walking first. Other possible starting points are shown on the map.

From Willerby Church we take the road through the village and then on through Staxton. A short stretch on the A64 then brings us to the round-about at (1). I don't recommend using the p.r.o.w. behind the café and through the caravans – I found the path unpleasant and overgrown.

turning sharp right and walking on the wide path between crops to Folkton Wold Farm.

After this, the path is clear at first but soon disappears in vegetation. There has been another diversion from that shown on the O.S. map and so we now stay next to the field boundary on our right until we reach the stile at (4). This is the point we reached on the last walk in order to complete the LPC link.

At the stile we turn right as we rejoin the WW/CW for the next 4.5 miles. Once again the waymarked route is easy to follow. We gain good views of typical rolling chalk country; Raven Dale and Lang Dale are fine examples of dry valleys which are too steep for easy ploughing and so remain as pasture. Apart from a short road section (5) we follow a wide path by field edges.

After we have slithered down into Cotton Dale Slack (6) we go right and take the more solid track up past Staxton Wold R.A.F. Station ... from all the notices, one gets the impression that curious walkers might not be altogether welcome. At the junction (7) we turn left on the narrow tarred road and walk on a gradual downslope to Staxton Wold Farm and the B1249. (Those doing the short walk can turn right here back to their car park.)

Fingerposts continue to direct us around field sides along the WW/CW and then at (8) we follow a pleasant hedged, sunken path down the chalk face. However, where the WW/CW bears left (9), we carry straight on to the A64. Turning right at the road, we walk on the pavement, past Willerby Wold Piggeries, as far as the track crossing at (10) just after Ganton Service Station. Going left through the gate, we arrive back at Willerby Church.

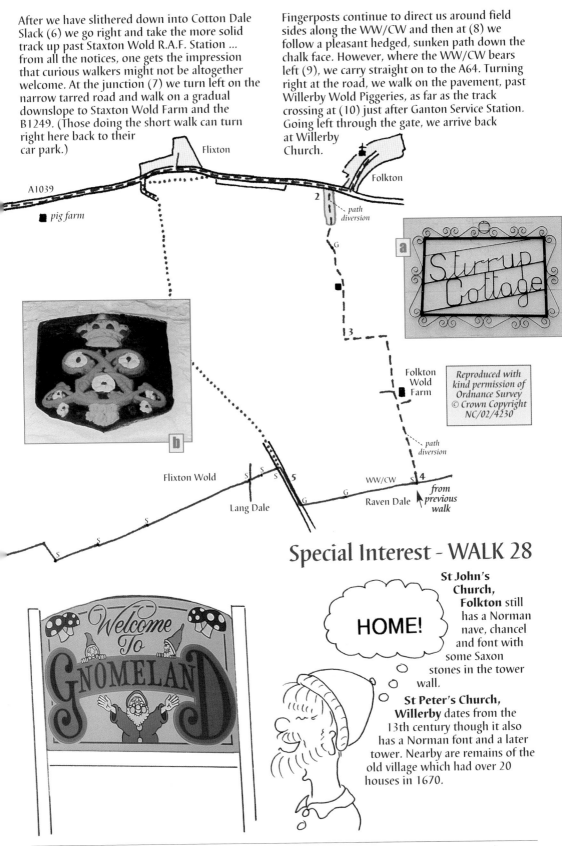

Flixton

A1039

pig farm

Folkton

2

path diversion

G

a

Sturrup Cottage

3

Folkton
Wold
Farm

path diversion

b

Flixton Wold

S S S 5

Lang Dale

G

WW/CW S 4

Raven Dale

from previous walk

Special Interest - WALK 28

Welcome To GNOMELAND

HOME!

St John's Church, Folkton still has a Norman nave, chancel and font with some Saxon stones in the tower wall.

St Peter's Church, Willerby dates from the 13th century though it also has a Norman font and a later tower. Nearby are remains of the old village which had over 20 houses in 1670.

WALK 29
BINNINGTON BROW – SHERBURN

Map: Explorer 300
S.E.P.:   A64 lay-by (979772)
Lake Pickering distance: 4.1 miles
Circular walk distance: 9.3 miles
Shorter walk alternatives: 4.5 miles;
                              5.4 miles

Although there two short sections along the A64 road, we have the consolation of a tarred pavement all the way. The suggested start is from the lay-by (1) opposite the Farm Bakery. This allows two short circuits (or a figure-of-eight walk) to be completed by using the road up to Potter Brompton.

From the east end of the lay-by we walk in the Scarborough direction for 50m to the stile at the gap in the hedge. We go through the trees along the edge of Ganton golf course following the waymarks. This is a noticeably different landscape from that of other Wolds walks because here we see gorse scrub growing on the sandy golf course soil.

At (2) we need to watch for the waymark which sends us right alongside the hedge and towards the golf club house. We pass in front of this and, crossing the road, follow the fingerpost directing us round the edge of this part of the golf course. The track soon becomes clear and takes us to a clump of pine trees behind the 18th tee and behind the trees is a small gate (3) in the fence. Even if the path ahead across the grazing land is not too obvious, we aim due east directly towards Windle Beck Farm. In the corner of the field just before the farm, we turn right on to the track taking us through three gates and the farmyard to the A64.

Going left we use the pavement for 500m before turning off right on to Wold Lane, the wide grassy track we used in the opposite direction on the previous walk. At (4) we turn right as we join the WW/CW and for the next four miles we follow this route. It is again well-signed and should give no navigation difficulties. We go alongside intensively farmed land and as we pass through Ganton we can make the slight detour to our right to Ganton church.

Continuing on the WW/CW, there is then a short road stretch before we turn off right opposite the driveway to Ganton Hall (5). We reach the Potter Brompton road (6) where the short walk turns away right. Long walkers do a right-left shimmy and then continue straight on, probably being treated to a fine display of porcine antics as we pass by fields of squealing piglets.

When we reach the fingerpost at (7) we turn left up the gentle slope and then on entering the wood, continue round to our right through the trees. At a fork in the path (8) we bear right, soon coming to the edge of the wood and continuing a short distance to a small gate where we turn right. A pleasant path, hedged at first, takes us round to the road at (9).

Turning right we go down the hill and into Sherburn but in order to link up with the next walk we take the track left at (10). In Sherburn we cross the A64, walk straight ahead and see both the Methodist Church and St Hilda's Church before continuing to the path turn-off on our right at (11).

We follow this path over rich black-soiled farmland, noting that the p.r.o.w. at (12) is virtually non-existent on the ground. Right and left turns round a field which had turf grass in 2003 take us to the gap in the tree line at (13). Here we go right and walk past more turf back to the A64. Turning left, it is then 0.75 mile on the pavement back to the lay-by car park.

FREE RANGE EGGS

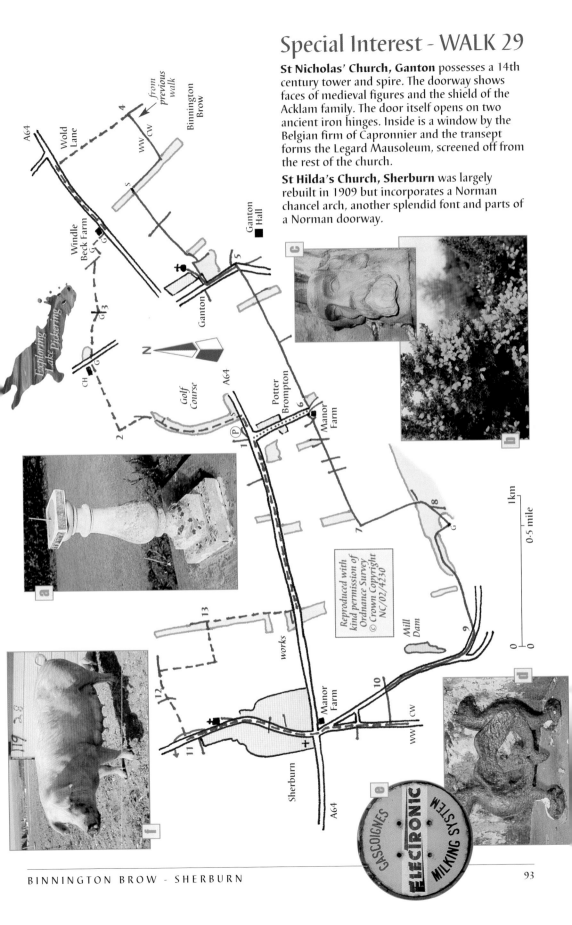

Special Interest - WALK 29

St Nicholas' Church, Ganton possesses a 14th century tower and spire. The doorway shows faces of medieval figures and the shield of the Acklam family. The door itself opens on two ancient iron hinges. Inside is a window by the Belgian firm of Capronnier and the transept forms the Legard Mausoleum, screened off from the rest of the church.

St Hilda's Church, Sherburn was largely rebuilt in 1909 but incorporates a Norman chancel arch, another splendid font and parts of a Norman doorway.

Reproduced with kind permission of Ordnance Survey © Crown Copyright NC/02/4350

WALK 30
SHERBURN –
EAST HESLERTON

Map: Explorer 300
S.E.P.: Sherburn (959769)
Lake Pickering distance: **2.4 miles**
Circular walk distance: **10.0 miles**
Shorter walk alternative: **7.0 miles**

The long walk contains a fair stretch of road but this is relatively quiet and does allow a good length circuit to be completed. If the shorter option is chosen, we miss the very attractive dry valley down Helperthorpe Slack. This route is a p.r.o.w. though it is not always clear on the ground.

Parking in Sherburn village, we cross the A64, walk south and then take the right fork (Whitegates) at (1). We follow this road, which soon becomes the Wolds Way, up the face of the chalk scarp to the old quarry (2). From here to the road junction at (3) the WW actually runs parallel to the tarmac but along the edge of the adjacent fields. We carry on to (4) and then turn sharp right off the road and for the next 1.5 miles follow the WW signposts directing us along the chalk scarp. There are a few turns but the route indicators are clear. As on the other stretches along this part of the Wolds Way, views down across the Vale are extensive.

On reaching the path crossing at (5) just before Manor Wold Farm, we leave the WW (though we shall continue along it on the next circular walk) and instead bear left to go through the farm. Then at the farmhouse itself, we turn left again to take the wide track southwards. This leads over more rich Woldian farmland to the road at (6) where there is yet another left turn.

At (7), just before East Heslerton Wold Farm, we have the choice of either taking the bridleway down through Helperthorpe Slack or continuing

on the road back towards Sherburn. If we decide on the first option, it is probably sensible to use the farm track along the edge of the first field and then turn right to the bottom of the dry valley. Turning left, we cross one more field to (8) and from there the p.r.o.w. continues along the left side of the hedge to the Weaverthorpe road (9). Now we go left and follow the road to (10) where a bridleway bears off right from the tarmac. In the past this has been fenced off but it is a p.r.o.w. and leads us round the field edge to another minor road at (11). From there, we turn left and it's a short way back to Sherburn.

If we choose the shorter option, we follow the road from (7) as far as (3) and then turn off left on the bridleway down the chalk face. The p.r.o.w. is actually signposted through recently planted trees but an easier line to take might be to go through the gate immediately to the right and use the wide field edge left clear by the farmer. Once again the route is obvious and we go straight down over the lower slopes to the main A64 and then turn right into Sherburn.

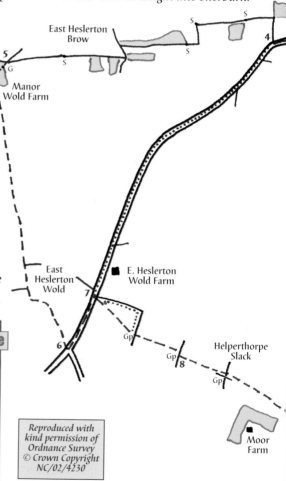

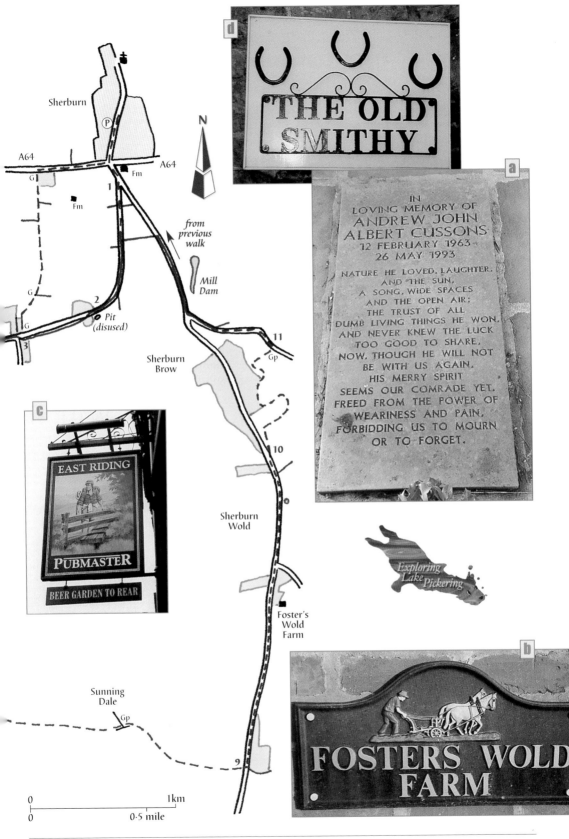

d THE OLD SMITHY

a
IN
LOVING MEMORY OF
ANDREW JOHN
ALBERT CUSSONS
12 FEBRUARY 1963 –
26 MAY 1993

NATURE HE LOVED, LAUGHTER,
AND THE SUN,
A SONG, WIDE SPACES
AND THE OPEN AIR;
THE TRUST OF ALL
DUMB LIVING THINGS HE WON,
AND NEVER KNEW THE LUCK
TOO GOOD TO SHARE.
NOW, THOUGH HE WILL NOT
BE WITH US AGAIN,
HIS MERRY SPIRIT
SEEMS OUR COMRADE YET.
FREED FROM THE POWER OF
WEARINESS AND PAIN,
FORBIDDING US TO MOURN
OR TO FORGET.

c EAST RIDING · PUBMASTER · BEER GARDEN TO REAR

b FOSTERS WOLD FARM

Sherburn

A64 · A64

Fm

G

Fm

1

from previous walk

Mill Dam

2

G

Pit (disused)

G

3

Sherburn Brow

11

Gp

10

Sherburn Wold

Exploring Lake Pickering

Foster's Wold Farm

Sunning Dale

Gp

9

N

0 ——— 1km
0 ——— 0·5 mile

WALK 31
EAST HESLERTON – KNAPTON PLANTATION

Map: Explorer 300
S.E.P.: East Heslerton Church (926767)
Lake Pickering distance: **2.3 miles**
Circular walk distance: **10.2 miles**
Shorter walk alternative: **6.7 miles**
    (returning via West Heslerton)

This walk takes us up the scarp face of the Wolds on to East and West Heslerton Wolds. There is some road walking but this is along quiet country lanes.

There is room for car parking outside East Heslerton Church and we start from here. Walking westwards away from the church, we turn left on the farm track leading up to the chalk escarpment. An information board tells us that we are passing what was probably a medieval village and we see evidence of this, perhaps, in the hummocky nature of the ground on our left.

The steep face of the scarp has been left to rough pasture and there is a fair covering of hawthorn scrub. We pass one of a number of disused chalk pits and cross one of several old earthworks before we meet the Wolds Way near the top of the ridge (1). Going over a stile on our right, we cross to the corner of the trees and then follow the WW/CW with the trees of Manor Wold Farm on our left. Visibility permitting, we get good views across 'Lake Pickering'.

We stay on the WW for about 2.5 miles, going round three sides of the trees at (2) and then alongside Abbey Plantation until we enter the woods of Knapton Plantation (3). The path continues just inside the trees and soon we come to the junction at (4). Those preferring the short walk now turn right on the track down through the trees to the A64 and then follow the road to West Heslerton from where the route continues eastwards to Rectory Farm.

The long walk turns left at (4) and goes up the gentle slope. At the top we turn left and use the wide farm track to go past South Farm and East Farm to the road at Wold Farm (5).

Now follows 1.2 miles of quiet road as we turn right and continue to the bridleway crossing at (6). We turn left on the grass-verged track towards Ling Hall Farm. Then immediately after the second clump of trees (7) we leave the track and follow the p.r.o.w. which branches off to our right and follows the field edge on the left side of the hedge. Approaching Whin Moor Farm, we pass between the older and newer tree plantations and skirt round to the road at (8). Going left, a short tarred stretch brings us to the junction at (9).

Taking a left turn, we now follow in the opposite direction the wide track used on the previous walk. When we come to Manor Wold Farm, we turn right and go back to the path junction (1) we reached earlier in the day.

There is now a choice. We can carry on and retrace our steps down the chalk face directly into East Heslerton. Alternatively, if we opt for a slightly longer route, we go over the stile on our left again, cross the field and continue westwards on the Wolds Way. About 100m after the end of the trees on our left, the p.r.o.w. branches off to our right. The path is not obvious but we aim for the stile which we can see. Then we go diagonally down the scarp, through the hawthorn bushes, to the stile in the far corner of the pasture (the line of trees acts as a guide) and then round the hillock in the next field to the gate by the disused chalk pits (10).

A clearer track now leads us round to Rectory Farm and at the end of the buildings we turn sharp left and continue to the stile at (11). Crossing this, we keep to the field edge on our right and follow Ass Beck as far as a small footbridge. (This section may be overgrown, so leggings could be useful protection against nettles.) Going over the bridge and stile, we then walk by the hedge back into East Heslerton.

Special Interest – WALK 31

St Andrew's Church, East Heslerton was built in 1877 for Sir Tatton Sykes by A.G.Street and is reckoned to be one of his finest churches. The tower is decorated with four large statues intended for Bristol Cathedral. The detailing of the interior screens, vaults and baptistry, with Street's use of fine marbles, exhibits Victorian craftsmanship at its best. The church is now sadly out of use.

All Saints Church, West Heslerton was rebuilt in the 19th century but the early English chancel from the 13th century contains an Easter sepulchre with sculpture showing the Coronation of the Virgin Mary.

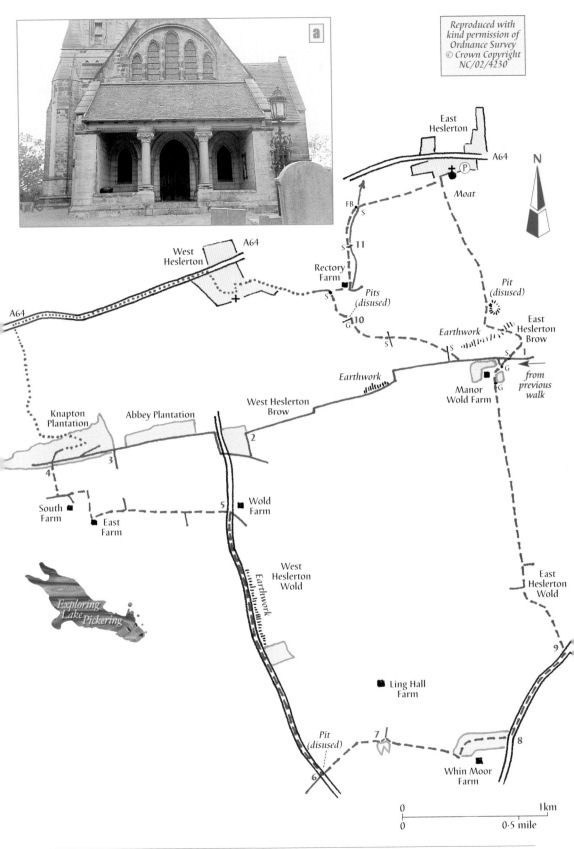

East
Heslerton

A64

Moat

N

FB

S

S — 11

West
Heslerton

A64

Rectory
Farm

Pits
(disused)

Pit
(disused)

East
Heslerton
Brow

A64

S

G — 10

Earthwork

S

S

S

1

Manor
Wold Farm

G

G

from
previous
walk

Earthwork

West Heslerton
Brow

Knapton
Plantation

Abbey Plantation

2

3

4

South
Farm

East
Farm

5

Wold
Farm

West
Heslerton
Wold

Earthwork

East
Heslerton
Wold

Exploring
Lake
Pickering

9

Ling Hall
Farm

Pit
(disused)

7

8

6

Whin Moor
Farm

0   1km

0   0·5 mile

WALK 32
KNAPTON PLANTATION - THORPE BASSETT

Map: Explorer 300
S.E.P.: West Knapton (875754) or
      Wintringham Church (887731)
Lake Pickering distance: **3.6 miles**
Circular walk distance: **9.2 miles**
Shorter walk alternatives: **5.7 miles;**
                          6.0 miles
Special interest: Scampston Hall

This walk includes a short stretch along the A64 but a tarred pavement allows safe walking. The recommended start is from the large lay-by at the A64-B1258 junction.

We walk along the road in an easterly direction, past the horse gallops on our left, to West Knapton and note the old pinfold as we turn back left towards the village. Very quickly we take the kissing gate on our right to go across ploughland and then through more kissing gates which indicate the p.r.o.w. over the open parkland of Knapton Hall to the minor road at (1). At this point there is a disappointment. Unfortunately the p.r.o.w. shown on the O.S. map cannot be used because when it comes to Mill Grange Farm, there is no legal exit on to main A64 road. We must therefore take the minor road to the A64 and then, turning left, use the pavement as far as the bridleway at (2).

Now we turn right and gradually rise towards the chalk scarp face of Knapton Grits. When we reach Knapton Plantation, we enter a delightful woodland. Many of the trees are beech which form a typical 'hanger' on the steep chalk face and afford pleasant shade if it is a hot day. At the track junction (3), we go more or less straight ahead following the waymark. We continue climbing, forking right at (4). However, it's easy not to see the waymark about 250m further on at (5) and there is no obvious path from there up the hillside to the edge of the wood. But if we do miss this turn, we rejoin our route at (6) a bit further on.

From there we continue just inside the plantation. We soon turn left at (7), cross a small field and meet the Wolds Way. We carry on along an ancient earthwork and then, just before entering the woods, are treated in July to a gorgeous display of wild raspberries. The track down Deep Dale dry valley is very steep but we may be lucky and hear the distinctive call of the buzzards circling above. Acorn waymarks guide us to Wintringham.

Wintringham Church is, at the time of writing, threatened with closure but if the building is open it is well worth looking inside. From here,

our route goes along the field edge behind the village, then bends back left at the road (8) before cutting off right at (9). The bird hide and pond specially created for the Millennium give a fine excuse for a refreshment stop.

We keep on the WW for two fields but where the WW turns left on the road, we keep straight on ahead, keeping to the left of the hedge. At Thorpe Bassett we turn right, then left at the fork, call at the church and then follow the road to the bend at (10).

Here we leave the road and, taking the path straight ahead, walk by the side of the games field to the edge of Rillington. We carry on into the village to the A64 and should pay a visit to the Church to view the remnant of 12th century wall painting. Then we continue along the A64 in the Scarborough direction and take the path on our left just after the pub car park. This brings us to a horse meadow and we follow the fence to the far side of the field before turning sharp right (11). With the hedge on our left, we carry on over a track and another meadow to the stile at (12). Going left, we cross more parkland and follow the road through Scampston village.

At (13) the p.r.o.w. branches off right and we go around the back of the estate, past the vegetable garden, to the path turning at (14). We turn left over the stream and then walk through some fine old conifers. When we come to Park Plantation (15) we need to go to the far side of the trees and then walk along the field edge to the A64. A left turn brings us back to the cars.

Special Interest - WALK 32

St Edmund's Church, Knapton lies down the drive to Knapton Hall but is now out of use.

St Peter's, Wintringham, with its impressive tower and spire, is regarded as being especially important in this part of the Wolds. The Normans (again!) built the chancel. The arcades date from the 14th century, as do the yellow stained aisle windows with their 32 pictures of saints. Interesting furniture abounds: there are ancient carved screens, a 17th century poor box, a 1736 font cover and Jacobean pews. **All Saints, Thorpe Bassett** kept its Norman doorway and font in the restructuring of 1879-80 and possesses some 14th century glass. **St Andrew's, Rillington** has a 13th century font and an important medieval wall painting which shows the consecration of the church and the institution of Robert de Okham as first vicar in 1230.
St Martin's, Scampston was built for Colonel W. St Quintin of Scampston Hall in 1842. Some of the masonry from an earlier church has probably been re-used in the outside walls.

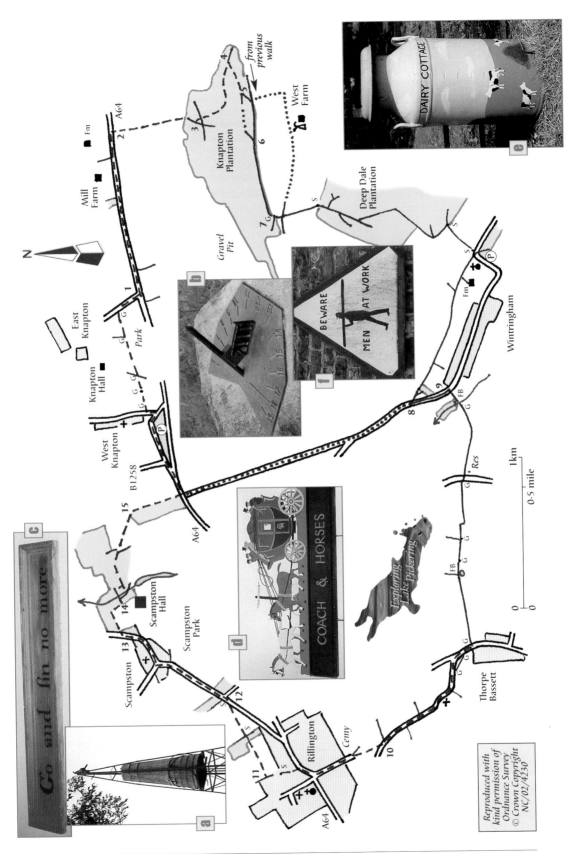

DAIRY COTTAGE

Go and fin no more

COACH & HORSES

BEWARE
MEN AT WORK

Exploring
Lake Pickering

Knapton Plantation

Deep Dale Plantation

from previous walk

West Farm

Gravel Pit

Mill Farm

Fm

A64

N

East Knapton

Knapton Hall

Park

West Knapton

B1258

A64

Scampston

Scampston Hall

Scampston Park

Rillington

Ceny

A64

Thorpe Bassett

Wintringham

Fm

Res

FB

0   0.5 mile   1km

WALK 33
THORPE BASSETT – SETTRINGTON

Map: Explorer 300
S.E.P.: Thorpe Bassett (862731)
Lake Pickering distance: **3.4 miles**
Circular walk distance: **11.1 miles**
Shorter walk alternatives: **7.7 miles;**
   3.8 miles

This walk takes us over undulating Wolds country with arable, pastoral and timber activities in evidence. There are two possible short-cuts available.

Leaving Thorpe Bassett we take the left fork by the Old School House at the end of the village and follow the road past Milbank House to the path turn off on our right (1). This leads us along a wooded ditch at the edge of intensively farmed fields to the stile at (2). Waymarks guide us round to the stile at (3) and now we aim for the corner of the wood up on our right and then there is a steep pull up to the gate at (4).

From here, the p.r.o.w. goes diagonally right (aim left of the telegraph pole) to a half-hidden stile and this takes us on to a wide bridleway. Turning left, we then pass to the *right* of the old building and the waymark directs us right again along the field edge. (The short walk goes straight ahead across Bassett Brow to Rowgate.)

After two fields we cross the road (5) and then use the signed diversion round Wold House. The path is a bit indistinct but we go down the slope and to the left of the two clumps of trees. Then we cross a rough grazing field to a gate in the fence (6) where the waymark directs us right. But don't bear too far right; if you hit the fence, follow it round left to the gate in the field corner and then cross over the small stream. From here there are several animal tracks going off left; the central ones approximate to the p.r.o.w. and we follow these to the gate at (7). At this point we observe the old ash tree on our left; one of the numerous points on the estate where barn owls are nesting.

Navigation is easier from now on. A broad track takes us to the road (8) and soon we pass the path at (9). Those preferring the medium length walk now turn off left and follow the waymarked route to the Screed Plantation. The longer walk carries on, past Settrington House, to the road junction at (10). Turning left, we now join the CW and continue to Station House where another left turn takes us to Kirk Hill.

We pass in front of the buildings but we immediately leave the main track and take the stile down to the footbridge over Settrington Beck. The path follows this clear meandering stream to North Grimston. (If there are bulls in the field, it may be sensible to use the edge of adjacent fields.)

A quick diversion right allows us to see the church, before we continue on the road through the village and admire the creative talents of generations of blacksmiths. Just after the pub the road can be dangerous, so we go quickly to the tarmac track at (11). This leads us over Whitestone Beck and up to rejoin the CW (now also the Wolds Way) and on through Wood House farmyard.

We carry on to the stile at (12) where the official Wolds Way path runs just inside the fence boundary. After a left-right turn (13) the wide track runs alongside the Screed Plantation and past High Bellmanear to the radio mast and 'raised reservoir' on the roadside. Selective felling of the trees ahead of us gives a pleasant change of scenery as we pass through the wood and bend round to the track junction at (14). Here we have to turn sharp left and then suddenly emerge from the trees to be given a fine view of 'Lake Pickering'. If we are lucky, we may see buzzards overhead.

A grassy path takes us down the scarp but when the WW turns off right (15), we carry on ahead for about 200m to the gate on our right and here take the p.r.o.w. diagonally across the field to the gap in the corner by Rowgate Farm. The farm track bears left, then bends sharp right and carries on for another mile back into Thorpe Bassett.

Special Interest - WALK 33

St Nicholas' Church, North Grimston is another Norman building with a magnificent early Norman font formed from a colossal 'drum' of limestone. It is one of four carved fonts on the Wolds; this one shows Jesus eating supper with his disciples and also depicts the descent of Jesus from the cross.

Ironwork – North Grimston is known for two sets of ironwork – the sword found here and associated with the Iron Age Parisii culture and the two horseshoe 'trees' located at the village forge.

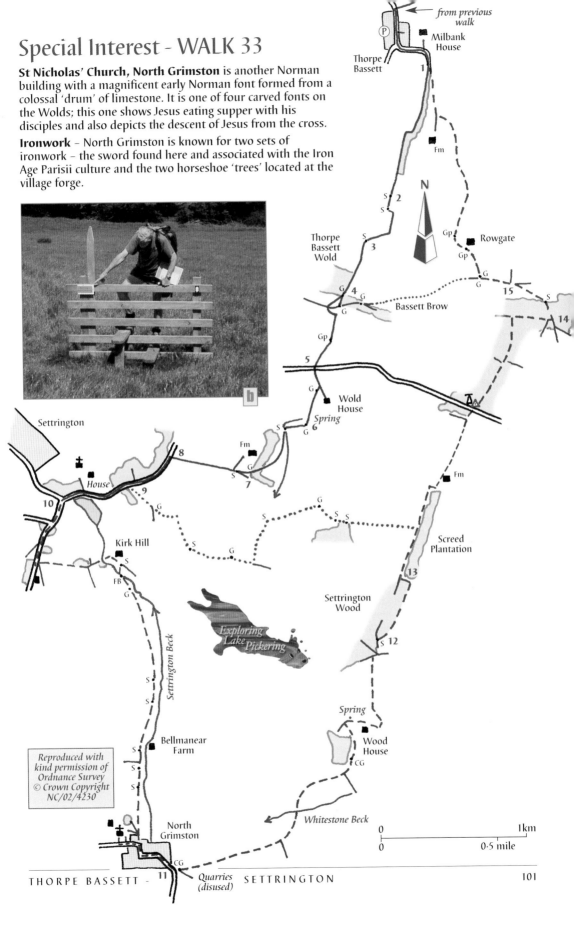

from previous walk

Milbank House

Thorpe Bassett

P

1

Fm

S 2
S

Thorpe Bassett Wold

S
3

N

Gp
Rowgate
Gp

G
15
S

G
4 G
G
Bassett Brow

14

Gp

5

G
Wold House
Spring
S
6 G

Settrington

8
Fm
G
S
7

Fm

House
9
G

10
G

Kirk Hill
S

FB
G

Screed Plantation

13

Settrington Wood

G
S S S
S
G
S
G

Exploring Lake Pickering

S 12

Settrington Beck

S

S

Bellmanear Farm
S

S

S

Spring

Wood House
CG

Reproduced with kind permission of Ordnance Survey © Crown Copyright NC/02/4230

North Grimston

CG

Whitestone Beck

11

Quarries (disused)

0   1km
0   0.5 mile

WALK 34
SETTRINGTON – NORTON

Map: Explorer 300
S.E.P.: Settrington Church (839702) or
      Langton Church (797671)
Lake Pickering distance: **4.3 miles**
Circular walk distance: **10.6 miles**
Special interest:
    Horse Racing *(this walk and the next walk)*

On this walk we first look at Settrington before going to the outskirts of Norton and then completing a square across farmland and horse racing country back to Settrington. The going, as they say, is generally good.

Starting from Settrington Church we walk NW towards the village, go first left down to the beck and then turn right alongside the stream to the footbridge (1). We cross to the opposite side of the water and walk to the road. A left turn takes us past the school and village hall, then bearing right, we skirt the Town Green and go to the end of the village (2).

Our route continues on the track going straight ahead and for the next mile or so we follow Centenary Way indicators. The path is soon swallowed up among trees (3) and when it emerges we need to look for the waymarks which show a slight diversion around the edge of the field before we come to the footbridge over the ditch at (4). Crossing the ditch, we climb up on to the old railway embankment and follow this as far as the path crossing at (5). It is important not to miss this; the main track continues ahead but we go down left off the banking and then take the half-hidden gap in the trees on our right.

We cross the stile at (6) and, turning left, keep to the field edge before being forced to turn right along the hedge. From here the path over farmland is clear to Beverley Road (B1248) at (7). Turning left, we continue to the fingerpost at (8) and here go right along the bridleway to Langton Road (9).

A quick right-left turn takes us into Bazley's Lane and then at (10) we turn left past Spring Cottage Stables. At the end of the lane we go through the hedge and then up right on to the main track. From here we walk more or less due south for two miles to Langton. Now is an opportunity to observe some of the variations of Woldian farming: intensive cereal cultivation, crop diversification (one field was a mass of blue borage when I came) and intensive pig production.

Langton may be a good place to picnic and certainly the church should be visited. We walk through the village and then continue eastwards for another couple of miles along Cordike Lane which, though tarmacked, is not a busy road. Going over the crossroads at (11) we carry on to the junction at (12). Turning left, we now complete the last leg of the walk back to Settrington.

After passing through a road service area, the path goes up through trees, cool and refreshing, or overgrown and damp, depending on the weather and the time of year. But soon the track widens out and runs between lines of trees, past the Langton Gallops, and down to Beverley Road. We cross straight over and continue along Langton Lane, another pleasant, tree-lined track, to the crossroads at (13). Here we go right for a mile on the road to Settrington and the side lane at (14) takes us back to the Church.

Special Interest – WALK 34

Settrington is a good example of an estate village which saw radical changes around 1800. The water mill was reconstructed, as was the manor house, and the old timber-framed village houses rebuilt in Jurassic limestone.

All Saints Church, Settrington has a fine large nave with 13th century arcades and rectangular font. There is a little ancient glass in one of the south aisle windows.

St Andrew's Church, Langton was largely rebuilt in 1822 but kept its 13th century font, some Jacobean panelling in the chancel and a splendid monument to Mrs Ingram who died in 1656.

Horse Racing is a major industry in this area and on this walk and the next we pass a number of racing stables. Whitewall Stables (Walk 35) is one of the best-known centres and in the 19th century John Scott was responsible for turning out a record 40 classic race winners from Whitewall. In those days all the horses had to be walked to the races and then walked back again. They travelled in long 'strings' with accompanying jockey lads, stopping off for rests and training gallops on the way. In 1836 John Scott sent a filly named Cyprian to take part in the Epsom Oaks. She won the race and was then promptly marched back to compete in the Northumberland Plate at Newcastle ... she won that race too! So as well as winning a classic and a tough handicap, Cyprian had finished a 500-mile walk in just a couple of months.

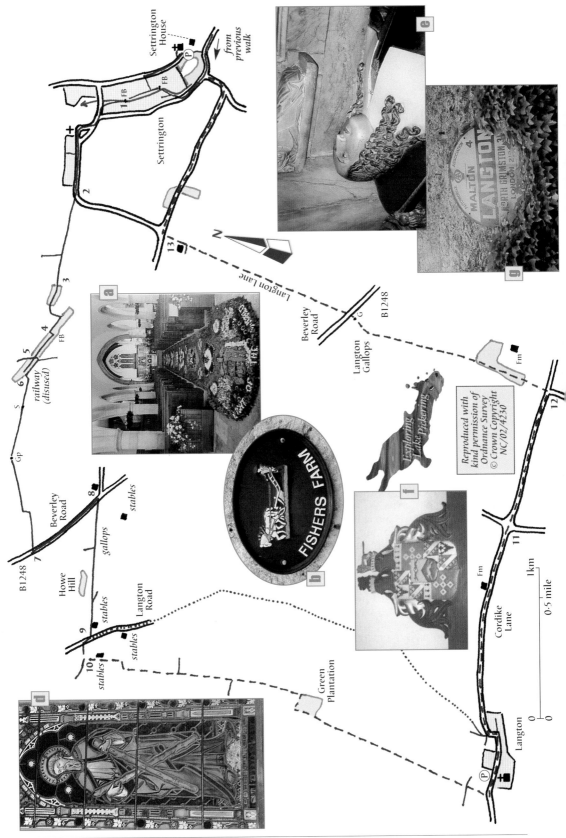

Settrington House

Settrington

from previous walk

Langton Lane

B1248
Beverley Road

Langton Gallops

Exploring Like Pickering

Reproduced with kind permission of Ordnance Survey © Crown Copyright NC/02/4230

railway (disused)

Gp

B1248
Beverley Road

Howe Hill

stables

gallops

Langton Road

stables

stables

stables

Green Plantation

FISHERS FARM

Fm

Cordike Lane

Langton

Fm

0   0·5 mile
0   1km

WALK 35
NORTON – MALTON –
LOW HUTTON

Map: Explorer 300
S.E.P.:   Malton (787719) or
         Low Hutton (762677)
Lake Pickering distance: **8.2 miles**
   (incl Malton loop)
Circular walk distance: **12.1 miles**
   (incl Malton loop)
Alternative walk: **9.1 miles**
   (excl Malton loop)
Shorter walk: **6.0 miles**
   (via Menethorpe Lane)
Special interest:
   Malton Town Trail, Derventio Roman
   Camp, Racing stables

This section of the LPC goes round the SW edge of Norton and then follows the Centenary Way along the River Derwent to Low Hutton. A highly recommended extra loop includes Old Malton and (New) Malton, though if preferred, this may be done as a separate Town Trail.

The route description assumes we park in Low Hutton village and complete the Malton loop in the middle of the walk. We leave the village to pass under the railway bridge and then over the River Derwent on the narrow pedestrian suspension bridge ... don't march in military unison or the resonance may cause panic!

A permissive path then takes us to Menethorpe hamlet and, bearing left up the road, we walk for 120m to the bridleway at (1). The short walk carries on straight ahead but the long walk takes the bridleway. Fingerposts direct us to the minor road (2) where, turning right, we continue for 150m to re-connect with the bridleway on our left. This takes us past Manor Farm, over another minor road and through four gates to Thornthorpe House. Passing left of the buildings, we turn sharp right and then at the end of the buildings need to veer slightly left on a faint path over the rough grass and down to the gate in the far left corner. We soon arrive at the track T-junction (3). Here we turn left and retrace, in the reverse direction, the route we followed on the last walk.

Just past Spring Cottage Stables (4) we join the main LPC route and go left on the road to Whitewall Stables (5). Then we turn right on to Welham Road and walk as far as the driveway to the golf club (6). We follow this drive, go right over the stile at the end and then take the path round to Star Cottage Stables (7). Now we follow stiles over a large paddock, across an arable field, alongside some allotments and then, bending right, emerge once on to Welham Road (8).

Turning left, we follow the road to the railway level crossing. Immediately after the crossing, those preferring not to do the Malton loop go left down Norton Road and follow the river. Alternatively, those wishing to include the loop cross the river and then take the first road right to Orchard Fields, the site of the Roman fort of Derventio.

Malton loop – At Orchard Fields we choose the right-hand path of the three in front of us and then, bearing slightly right at the old railway embankment, we soon come to the banks of the Derwent. We now follow a muddy path to the kissing gate at (9) and then, keeping the Cut ditch on our left, continue on the permissive path to the Priory Church of St Mary, Old Malton.

After visiting the church we leave by the main driveway to Malton Road and then turn left towards (New) Malton. Opposite the Ryedale Council offices (10) we bear diagonally left over an arable field, cross the rail embankment and then come to the Roman Camp again.

We should certainly spend some time here before rejoining Malton Road and following part of the Town Trail, noting a number of historic buildings each with its own descriptive wall plaque. After passing The Lodge and St Leonard's Church, we turn right at the traffic lights into Wheelgate. Amongst the shops we see the Crown Hotel, with its on-site brewery. Here is produced Double Chance bitter, named after a 1920s Grand National winner once stabled in the present brewhouse. Then we pass the Cross Keys pub, whose vaulted cellars may have been a hospice linked to St Mary's Abbey, before turning left up Finkle Street. This leads us to the Museum, housed in the old Town Hall, and then to St Michael's Church. Continuing down Market Street, we turn left at Yorkersgate, then first right down Railway Street to cross the River Derwent over Iron Bridge. An abrupt right turn takes us back on to the Centenary Way running alongside the river.

Navigation is now easy; we just keep to the riverside all the way back to Low Hutton.

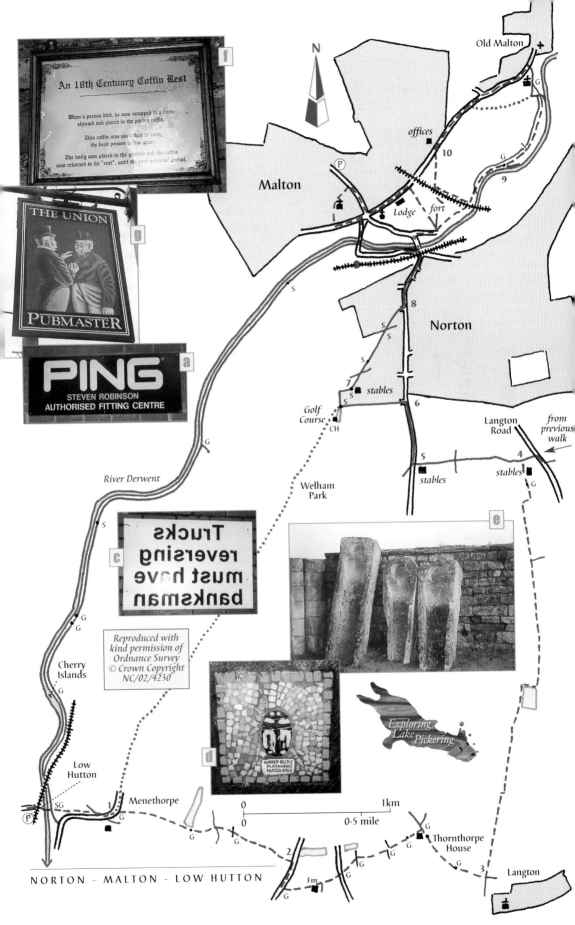

An 18th Century Coffin Rest

When a person died, he was wrapped in a linen shroud and placed in the parish coffin.

This coffin was used then to carry the dead person to his grave.

The body was placed in the ground and the coffin was returned to its "rest", until the next persons' burial.

f

THE UNION
PUBMASTER

g

PING
STEVEN ROBINSON
AUTHORISED FITTING CENTRE

a

N

Old Malton

Malton

offices

10

9

Lodge   fort

P

Norton

8

S

S
S

S

7   stables

S
S

6

Golf
Course
CH

Langton
Road

from
previous
walk

5   4

stables   stables

G

Welham
Park

River Derwent

S

Trucks
reversing
must have
banksman

c

Reproduced with
kind permission of
Ordnance Survey
© Crown Copyright
NC/02/4230

G
G

Cherry
Islands

G

e

WATER BEETLE
PLATAMBUS
MACULATUS

d

Exploring
Lake Pickering

Low
Hutton

SG

P

1   Menethorpe

G

G

Thornthorpe
House

G

Langton

0   1km
0   0.5 mile

NORTON - MALTON - LOW HUTTON

2

Fm
G

G   G

G

3

Malton

Derventio Roman Camp had an unusually big fort and it has been suggested that it may have been used as a storage centre for the large supplies of grain from the surrounding countryside. The civil settlement ('vicus') which served the fort grew up to the south and was a relatively sophisticated settlement, some buildings having their own water supplies and latrines. One building even had under-floor and wall heating. On the south (Norton) side of the river a major pottery industry was established. Long after the Romans departed, a Norman motte and bailey castle was built over one corner of the fort. This was then later replaced by a Jacobean Mansion and the remains of this can be seen today at The Lodge.

All that is left of **Old Malton Priory Church,** founded in 1150, is the nave, but that is impressive enough. One of the two western towers has gone and the entrance to the church is through a splendid late Norman doorway. Inside the only part of the south aisle that remains is under the tower. Otherwise, the arcades date from the late Norman period to the end of the Middle Ages. A few of the misericords remain in the chancel stalls. A walk round the outside of the church allows us to see the crossing piers at the east end as well as to gain some idea of the huge size of the original church. A few remnants of the monastic buildings exist under the adjacent Abbey House.

St Michael's, Malton was founded in the market place around 1150 as a chapel of ease for Old Malton. The arcades are from the 12th century, though the tower is later.

St Leonard's, Malton, now the Roman Catholic church in the town, was also built as a chapel of ease for Old Malton. Arcades date from the 12th century and a brass memorial to John Gibson (died 1837) shows the iron-founder at both prayer and bottle, with an exhortation to copy his virtues and to shun his vices.

Jeffry Bog comprises two fields of relic wetland pasture rich in flowering plants. Yellow irises are abundant and we should look for the spectacular ant hills in the reserve's north west corner. The adjacent Jeffry Bog Plantation is not part of the reserve.

Manor Farm is a 'LEAF' Farm (Linking Environment And Farming) venture and is a fine example of how agriculture and nature can work together in harmony. In the short time since 1998 when 'environmentally friendly' practices were adopted, there has been an impressive list of achievements:

- the farm's breeding wild bird population has increased by 50% and tree sparrows, a species in serious decline in the country as a whole, have increased from two pairs to 30 pairs
- 22 species of butterfly, including the relatively rare clouded yellow and marbled white, are now resident
- since hedge-cutting is now carried out less frequently, sloe berries (from the blackthorn) are now actually a profitable economic crop being gathered for making into sloe gin and sloe chocolate (yes, honestly!).

It is suggested that a good time to visit the farm is in midsummer when the flowering meadows, which have replaced some of the wheat fields, are in full bloom and provide a variety of nectar and pollen sources for insects. Phone 01653 617352 for details.

St Mary's, Westow is yet another church which, apart from the tower, was rebuilt by the Victorians. However, the Norman font can still be seen, as can a 12th century carving of the crucifixion on a 'cresset' stone in the west wall. Check before visiting because the church's isolation from the village means it is not always open.

Leavening Chapel has the distinction of having been converted from the old village school room.

All Saints Church, Burythorpe, 'The Church on the Hill', stands imposingly in its circular churchyard. It has been suggested that this was a pre-Christian site of pagan worship. The present building was erected on the site of its predecessor in 1865. Electricity has recently been supplied to the church but the old gas lighting system has been retained.

The Manor Farm Project

A major part of the Project's policy has been to create 'sown perennial margins'. This means sowing a mixture of grasses or grasses and wildflowers around the edges of fields in order to provide pollen and nectar sources for various insects. In addition this can give protective cover to small mammals.

On other parts of the farm areas of set-aside are left uncultivated in order to encourage 'arable weeds' (important 'wild flowers' to the conservationist!). Manor Farm is now probably Yorkshire's most important location for the rare Prickly Poppy weed.

On the farm 84 bird species have been recorded. One means of attraction has been to provide winter feeding material and 'tailcorn' – floor sweepings and waste grain – is spread on farm tracks during the winter. Experiments sowing different mixtures of wildbird cover crops such as kale, millet, teasel and linseed are also being monitored.

Sunny, sheltered, grassy margins generally provide the best habitats for butterflies and the marbled white seems to prefer tall grass.

Bumblebees provide an essential pollination service for many cultivated as well as wild plants. Of a total of 19 known bumblebee species, Manor Farm has all six of those which are commonly found in the U.K. Red clover, grown in the grass and wildflower plots, is believed to be a particularly good source of nectar and pollen.

Barn owls have declined in the U.K. for various reasons. For example, an estimated 4,000 are killed or maimed every year on our roads. Manor Farm has successfully undertaken a Barn Owl Release Programme and these birds are now resident on the farm.

The Manor Farm Project would seem to offer exciting prospects for the future development of British farming.

Information and photographs on this page have been kindly supplied by the Farmed Environment Company.

WALK 36
LOW HUTTON – KIRKHAM PRIORY

Map: Explorer 300
S.E.P.: Low Hutton (762677) or
Kirkham Priory (735658) or
Leavening (794632)

Lake Pickering distance: **3.5 miles**
Circular walk distance: **13.0 miles**
Shorter walk alternatives: **8.8 miles;**
7.3 miles

Special interest:
Manor Farm, Jeffry Bog

The last section of the LPC follows the Centenary Way from Low Hutton to Kirkham Priory. As for the last walk, we park in Low Hutton and cross the suspension bridge but this time turn immediately right over a small footbridge and then the CW path takes us up to the road at (1). Another right turn allows us good views of the peaceful Derwent as we follow the road to the junction at (2) and then, turning right, continue to the path turn-off at (3). This takes us back to the riverside and the Jeffry Bog marsh (an SSSI). We go left at the river and though the path can be squelchy it has recently been improved with boardwalks and small footbridges.

Turning left at the finger post (4) we walk up into Coldwell Plantation. We are careful here; at the gate we follow the waymarked CW route up the steep banking on the left (not the p.r.o.w. shown on the O.S. map). This then follows the field side until we turn sharp right (5) on the farm track to the metalled road at Firby. Here we go right at the first T-junction, turn quickly left into the drive to Firby Hall and then we are immediately directed right. Tall white markers direct us over four stiles and gates. At the last of these (6) the p.r.o.w. goes across the ploughed

land to the gate on the roadside. Then turning right, we are soon back in Kirkham.

To complete the circular walks, we return up the Langton road as far as Dark Lane (7) and turn right up this hedged track which later becomes a fieldside path and brings us to Westow. We turn left then right to walk through the village before going left again (8) on the Burythorpe road. At the end of the houses (9) the short walk continues round the left bend in the road and then turns left on the road signposted to the church. The longer walks bear right on the grassy track called High Lane which later narrows to a secretive sunken path before coming to the road at (10).

Those doing the medium length walk turn left to Manor Farm (15) while the long walk turns right, then quickly left at the lay-by, on to another wide hedged track (Hanging Hill Lane). This leads up and round to the minor road at (11). Here we turn left and walk into and through Leavening. At the far end of the village, we stay on the main road and, bearing left up the hill, come to the road junction at (12), just before the picnic site.

Going through the gate on our left, we follow the track swinging round right to another gate

---

but rather than going through this gate, we bend left down the slope on an unmarked p.r.o.w. After about 35m we avoid the temptation to veer right but follow the gulley going downslope. This soon becomes yet another double-hedged track and then a more open path as we follow it to Burythorpe. At the road we bear right and walk through the settlement until, just before the end, we go left on the side-road to All Saints Church. From there, the p.r.o.w. continues to the road (13) where we turn right to the sand works (14).

An industrial unit like this comes as a surprise in the rural environment but as we turn left at the end of the works, the honey-coloured piles of sand add a pleasing variation to the landscape. The route is slightly diverted around the potentially dangerous quarry and then we carry on to the road at (15). A right-left shuffle takes us on to the drive to Manor Farm and then just after the farm we bend right on a grassy track through the trees. At Ruffin Lane we turn left and then at the junction (2) a right turn takes us back to Low Hutton.

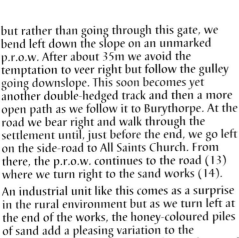

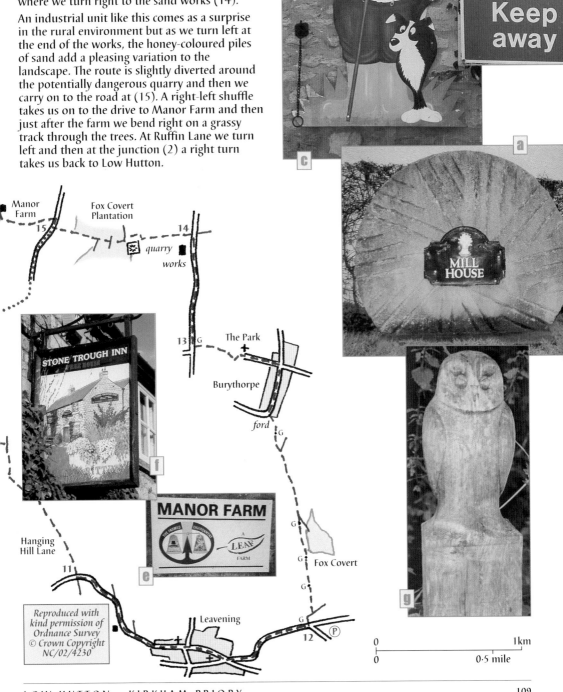

Reproduced with kind permission of Ordnance Survey © Crown Copyright NC/02/4230

Walk 36(a)
alternative route

This 7.0 miles circuit is an optional extra following the River Derwent from Kirkham Priory downstream to Howsham and back.

We cross the river over the ancient bridge and then immediately go left on to the riverside path. This leads us for three miles along the edge of the water all the way down to Howsham Bridge, the next crossing point over the river. As on the earlier riverside stretch, this section of the walk can be very boggy but some sections have been improved with duckboards and small footbridges.

When we come to the bridge we turn left on the road, then soon go left again into Howsham village. Just after the church, a finger post directs us right past Old Church Farm. Going through a series of small gates we then walk by the field edge to the stile at (1) and then, 30m further on, reach another stile. We now walk on the right side of the narrow belt of trees down to a fordable pond and up to the edge of Howsham Wood.

Entering the wood, we then follow the wide track up to the path crossing at (2). We may either use the old p.r.o.w going straight ahead or we can use the track cutting back sharp left. Both are delightful and take us through the mainly deciduous wood to the exit at Badger Bank where we bend left to come to the road corner (3). Continuing straight ahead on the road, we're soon in Kirkham.

St John's Church, Howsham, built by A.G. Street in 1860, has an unusual style and its rounded apse, bell cote and steep roof lend it something of an alpine appearance. Coloured marble stone increases its individuality.

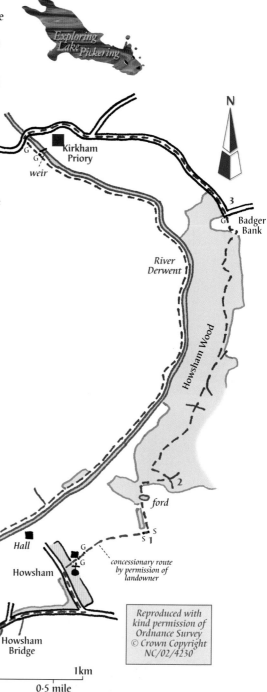

EXPLORING LAKE PICKERING

Appendix: LAKE PICKERING

The story of how the lakes in the Cleveland area developed was first described by Professor Percy Kendall in his classic study of 1902. The last of the four major advances of the ice during the Ice Age ended about 18,000 years ago and is known as the Devensian. However during this time the glaciers did not over-ride the North Yorkshire Moors. Instead northern ice sheets moved down southwards along both sides of the Moors (we know this from tracing the movement of erratic rocks such as Shap granite which were moved by the ice and then left in their new location where the glaciers melted) and as they did so they acted as enormous dams, trapping any meltwater streams and stopping them from escaping either to the North Sea or to the Vale of York. As a result large lakes were impounded by these ice dams. The biggest of the lakes were Lake Eskdale and Lake Pickering with another forming Lake Hackness (see map on page 4).

To the north side of the North York Moors, Kendall believed that several lakes had joined together to create Lake Eskdale, trapped by the ice-wall around present-day Whitby. This lake increased in size until it became so deep that it was able to escape by overflowing southwards over the lowest part of the plateau. This was at a point where Fen Bogs is now located. The torrent of water which moved south was so powerful that it eroded deep into the plateau surface to form the magnificent gorge of upper Newtondale. Then near Levisham station it joined the valley of a south-flowing stream and continued to race down to the Vale of Pickering. Here there was another lake and as the water from Newtondale entered Lake Pickering its speed was slowed down and a large lake delta of sediment was deposited. This provided a valuable raised site for the later building of Pickering above the marshy lower land of the flat Vale floor.

Further to the east, there developed a third lake known as Lake Hackness. Kendall believed that before the Ice Age a river valley existed along the line of what is now Troutsdale and the Sea Cut Valley and this carried water out to the North Sea. However, this valley became blocked by a wedge of ice and the evidence for this may be seen in the moraine left by the ice at Thorn Park (985882). With the Sea Cut outlet closed, water was trapped and Lake Hackness came into existence. As this lake increased size, it overflowed and escaped along the front edge of the ice sheet cutting the channel now known as Forge Valley down to East Ayton. Then the water is thought to have flowed west along the northern margin of the ice which had moved into the Vale of Pickering as far as Wykeham. Other steep-sided valleys like that of The Mere and Deepdale are also thought to have been ice-margin channels emptying into the Vale of Pickering as they flowed along the edge of the ice. So as the North Sea ice melted and the glacier retreated from its Wykeham position, the exposed area would have been filled with melt-water and either the main lake would have extended further eastwards or a separate lake would have formed.

At Wykeham the large moraine deposit dumped by the ice includes rocks carried down south from Durham and Northumberland and marks the limit of at least one stage of the ice movement. Except in the north (i.e., around Wykeham Park) the moraine today only has low height.

On the western side of the Vale of Pickering there is a large fault valley known as the Coxwold-Gilling Gap which gives access to the Vale of York. This gap was effectively plugged near Wass with a lobe of ice sent out from the main Vale of York glacier. So Kendall argued that between the ice plugs at Wykeham and Wass, Lake Pickering had been trapped. (The Wass ice lobe allowed meltwaters from the western side of the Cleveland Hills to be diverted through the fault trench and so into Lake Pickering.) At Crayeland Wood (561778) between Wass and Ampleforth the fault valley is partly obstructed by a hill made up largely of boulder clay thought to have been left by the ice.

The waters in Lake Pickering rose until they overtopped the watershed in the Howardian Hills, so this barrier was broken down and the lake waters plunged south to carve out another spectacular gorge, this time the Kirkham Gorge. This is the route used today by the River Derwent in its course from the North York Moors to the Ouse and then to the Humber Estuary.

Numerous modifications to Percy Kendall's theories have been suggested over the last 100 years. Working in Eskdale, K. J. Gregory (1965) argued that the isolated hills and ridges seen today could not have existed in a large lake but must have been formed in 'stagnant' ice. This is ice which was not moving but rather decayed gradually where it stood. The glaciers, he suspected, occupied considerably more of the valley, and the lake much less, than Kendall had believed.

Gregory's doubts about Lake Eskdale have caused geographers to be sceptical about the amount of meltwater which was ponded up as Lake Pickering and the precise extent of the Lake is a matter of speculation. But work by J. A. Catt (1987) shows that a temporary lake did form in the Vale.

As the ice melted, a separate lake known as Lake Flixton, blocked by boulder clay dumped along the North Sea coast, formed in the eastern part of the Vale. Lake Flixton has been the subject of much recent research and E. W. Cloutmann (1988) has shown that the edge of the lake followed the present 23 or 24 metre contour. The deepest water was in the area near Flixton and Star Carr and several mounds of glacial material formed islands in the lake. Today 'Lake Flixton' can be identified on the ground by its darker peat soils whilst the edge of the lake is marked by lighter sandy soils.

Churches in the following towns and villages will be visited on the inaugural walks on 10th May 2003.

Walk number

1	Welburn, Whitwell, Crambe
2	Coneysthorpe
3	Amotherby, Appleton-le-Street, Barton-le-Street, Slingsby
4	Hovingham, Terrington
5	Stonegrave, Nunnington
6	Gilling East. (Yearsley very close to the walk)
7	Coxwold, Ampleforth (Wass very close to the walk)
8	Oswaldkirk, Sproxton
9	Helmsley
10	Rievaulx, Old Byland
11	Pockley, Carlton
12	Beadlam, Kirkdale
13	Kirkbymoorside, Gillamoor
14	Appleton-le-Moors, Lastingham, Hutton-le-Hole
15	Sinnington, Cropton, Wrelton
16	Middleton
17	Pickering, Thornton-le-Dale, Ellerburn
18	Ellerburn
19	Allerston, Ebberston
20	Snainton, Wydale Hall
21	Brompton-by-Sawdon, Ruston, Wykeham, Hutton Buscel
22	Hackness, West Ayton
23	East Ayton
24	Scarborough
25	(Cayton close to walk)
26	Filey, Gristhorpe
27	Muston, Hunmanby
28	Folkton, Willerby
29	Ganton, Sherburn
30	Sherburn
31	East Heslerton (and alternative loop to West Heslerton)
32	Winteringham, West Knapton, Thorpe Bassett, Rillington, Scampston
33	North Grimston
34	Settrington, Langton
35	Old Malton, (New) Malton (Norton very close to walk)
36	Leavening, Burythorpe (alternatives to Westow and Howsham)